A SHORT HISTORY OF RELATIONS BETWEEN PEOPLES

A SHORT HISTORY of RELATIONS BETWEEN PEOPLES

How the world began to move beyond tribalism

JOHN M. ELLIS

BOOKS

NEW YORK • LONDON

Encounter Books
www.encounterbooks.com
© 2024 by John M. Ellis

First American edition published in 2024 by Encounter Books,
an activity of Encounter for Culture and Education, Inc.,
a nonprofit, tax-exempt corporation.
Encounter Books website address: www.encounterbooks.com

Manufactured in Canada and printed on acid-free paper.
The paper used in this publication meets the minimum requirements
of ANSI/NISO z39.48–1992 (R 1997) (Permanence of Paper).

LIBRARY OF CONGRESS CATALOGING-IN-PUBLICATION DATA IS AVAILABLE

Information for this title can be found at the Library of Congress
website under the following ISBN 978-1-64177-405-5 and LCCN 2024018111.

FIRST AMERICAN EDITION

Introduction

IN 1974, THE International Chess Federation adopted as its motto *gens una sumus*, the Latin phrase which means that we human beings are all of one family. It's easy to see how this idea applies to chess-players. The board makes everyone equal before its clearly defined rules. The players may speak different languages, but on the chessboard they all use the same idiom. Nationality, sex, skin color, temperament—all make no difference to what happens in the course of the game. Though *gens una sumus* has never been formally adopted by the United Nations, it's by now the unofficial ethos of that body, and the European Union committed to something very similar when in 1985 it adopted the "Ode to Joy," Beethoven's setting of Friedrich Schiller's early poem "An die Freude," as its anthem. Schiller's text includes the telling words: "Alle Menschen werden Brüder"—all men become brothers.

It's an attractive idea, and one that has been expressed at various times throughout history, but the widespread currency that it now enjoys is a recent phenomenon. It suggests that our commonality with other human beings goes deeper than any cultural or other differences between us. The cultures we grew up in may differ in all kinds of ways—from superficial customs like clothing to more profound matters such as morality and ethics—but we are still, first and foremost, fellow human beings. At least in the Western world, most people will now profess allegiance to this principle. Few will want to gainsay the basic idea that while the human family encompasses people of very different cultures and races, all people have a basic humanity in common, and as such are equally valuable and worthy of respect. Accordingly, most of us are now reluctant to say (at least publicly) that any one group is better or more deserving than another—or even that there are any truly fundamental differences between them. Anyone who says anything to the contrary must expect to be called a "racist." Indeed, the entire modern obsession with racism and anti-racism depends upon the assumptions implicit in the ideology of *gens una sumus*.

Nevertheless, there are times when this attitude seems not to work very well. Under the spell of its insouciant goodwill, we easily gloss over the fact that there are real and serious differences between peoples, that those differences are of a great many kinds, and that some of them do indeed demand resolute moral judgment. We have only to read Robert Edgerton's valuable book *Sick Societies*[1] to see that there is an enormous variety in human behavior, and that some societies exhibit an extreme of disfunction and cruelty that can make our generalized optimism about the common humanity of all people difficult to maintain. We are deluding ourselves, for instance, if we don't admit that we detest the Taliban because of their treatment of women. Many people still say openly that the Russian army is and has long been notorious for its exceptional brutality. That was the opinion of almost every Viennese woman I spoke to when I lived in Vienna in 1957, shortly after the Russian occupation of part of that city had ended. Is that characterization of an important Russian institution racist, or is it simply an opinion that either does, or doesn't, reflect reality, depending on the observed facts of the case? Does a commitment to *gens una sumus* mean that any attribution of a peculiar characteristic that begins "Chinese people are..." is racist? That's what some now seem to think, but surely that's a restriction on thought that leaves us without the ability to make judgments that can seem unavoidable.

In any case, for all its current prestige as an idea, it's safe to say that *gens una sumus* is not yet a belief system that is shared uniformly across the globe. China's leaders certainly appear to think that other peoples are not equal to the Chinese, and Vladimir Putin evidently thinks that the promotion of Russian ambitions justifies murdering the people of other countries by the tens of thousands. In parts of the Middle East, ancient tribal hatreds remain almost intact. And yet *gens una sumus* remains a worldwide public orthodoxy in the sense that even those whose actions betray the fact that they don't believe a word of it know that they must never say so in public. At least in the Western world, most people are now inclined to think that all peoples would be capable of the same sensible and responsible conduct that we expect of ourselves if the cultures they had grown up in hadn't predisposed them to behaviors that fall short of those expectations. That's certainly an admirable view in its way, even if it's sometimes hard to square with what really happens around the world.[2]

But whatever the limitations and inconsistencies of this apparent modern consensus, it is indisputable that even this incomplete accord has not been around for very long. The road that led to its current partial triumph was in fact long and hard. Those who write as if it had been the prevailing ethos in the early 17th century, as the "1619 Project" author Nikole Hannah-Jones does, are simply and hopelessly wrong.[3] In fact, it would be hard to find even a small number of people whose thought was guided by *gens una sumus* at that time. This was not because the people of that era were thoughtless and irresponsible. The reason was rather—as we'll see in the next chapter—that it would have been extremely foolish for them to have thought that way in those historical circumstances.

Nevertheless, most contemporary American academics now routinely use the modern standard of *gens una sumus* to judge historical figures as guilty of racism. It's as well to be clear about this: every accusation of racism, whatever the context in which it is made, depends on the assumption that the prevailing ethos of the time was *gens una sumus*, because where that ethos did not prevail the accusation makes no sense. Only when we believe that human beings are all of one family is it possible to violate that belief.

American higher education is currently obsessed with the way in which different groups of people looked at each other in the past, and with how they consequently mistreated each other—those groups being defined mostly by race. No issue now seems more ever-present than racism when our past is under scrutiny. It is now so central to historical studies that for many historians the whole point of historical exploration and analysis seems to be to convict people of former eras of racism. The accusations are often leveled at prominent historical figures, but they can be directed at almost anyone who has deviated from what current orthodoxy regards as correct thinking on racial matters.

It's occasionally said, and in one sense reasonably enough, that these academic historians are judging people of the past by modern standards, not by the standards of their own time. There is obviously some truth in this, but it's not an entirely convincing argument. It seems to concede the point that people of the past were morally inferior: they were, after all, willing to put up with ethical lapses that we won't now tolerate. This common defense of past societies therefore allows an easy rebuttal: if virtually everyone in those times was guilty of such thought and behavior, so much the worse for them. Theirs was, in that case, a bigoted age. Even after the objection that people of the past are being judged anachronistically, therefore, the practical result is that they are still left convicted of racism.

In the course of this book I'll try to show that this common defense of the past—that it can't be judged by modern standards—misses the real point. The way that different ethnic or national groups think about each other, and consequently treat each other, has changed profoundly over the last five hundred years, but not because we all became better people as time went by. Attitudes have changed because the conditions of life have changed. The attitudes that any one people had toward other peoples five hundred years ago were not free choices, in the sense that they could just as well have been different. To the contrary, they were inevitable given the conditions that prevailed in those times. And those conditions were never compatible with the ideology of *gens una sumus*.

When leftist scholars criticize the racism of earlier times, they essentially assume that our modern belief in *gens una sumus* is quite simply the natural one—the basic, expected standard, whatever the era under consideration. The truth is exactly the reverse of this. As we'll see, it's the *older* attitude that is the norm throughout the ages, while it's the modern attitude that is artificial, something that had to be learned. The proof of this is that even today, wherever that modern ethos has not been learned, its opposite (i.e., tribalism) always prevails, because it, not *gens una sumus*, is the more natural condition. In most historical contexts tribalism was a wise and prudent choice, and only the rapidly changing conditions of the last few centuries have made it feasible and sensible to depart from it. It can't therefore be regarded as a regrettable lapse from a self-evident norm, because it stood as the default condition of human history, until certain specific events began to change it. What exactly were those events? That question goes to the heart of this book. My purpose is to examine the key historical developments that altered how different peoples think about each other.

The road to the still somewhat imperfect modern consensus on *gens una sumus* is not one of a gradual growth with time, as is sometimes the case in history. To be sure, there are certain critical events in its evolution without which it could never have flourished, but those developments didn't just pop up randomly and then gradually grow stronger worldwide. Instead, they appear in specific places and among specific peoples, and then spread only to the extent that those peoples influenced other peoples. Moreover, progress toward *gens una sumus* doesn't always proceed in a straight line. On occasion, things appear to step backwards while laying the groundwork for the next forward move.

It's certainly true that, when confronting historical situations, none of us can completely suppress the urge to assess the rights and wrongs of what we see according to our own lights. Nonetheless, the tendency of many modern American historians to prioritize demonstrating the depravity of our national past is debilitating for all of us. Whether the people who are prominent in our national history were indeed guilty of racism or are instead falsely accused of it, the result is much the same: the constant obsession with the issue casts a shadow over the nation's history, one that is needless and groundless. What now makes matters even worse is that academia's determination to convict the nation's past as well as its present of moral obscenity has recently spilled over into the general population through the medium of elementary and high school teaching. Schoolchildren are being taught to apply a standard of judgment for periods in our nation's history when, for good reason, almost nobody would have entertained such judgments.

This study is therefore a history of how cultures looked at and thought about one another. There are good reasons to begin at the year 1500 AD, because that is when several key historical events begin to change what for millennia had been the way that almost every society thought about others. The year 1500 is thus the place where the road to modern attitudes begins. In one sense, this must be a history that is global in scope: it concerns how the world has changed in a certain crucial respect. On the other hand, we shall need to focus most on those peoples who were the agents of the change, because it was they who led the world in the direction of our modern outlook.

Chapter One: The World of 1500

WHY START THIS history at 1500 AD? Because it was at this point that a particular aspect of the human condition, one that had been relatively constant for thousands of years, was confronted by no less than three major developments that together initiated astonishingly far-reaching change. Just how those three factors operate will emerge in subsequent chapters, but I'll introduce them briefly now.

The first is the beginning of the Age of Discovery, which immediately brought into close and sustained contact peoples who had hitherto known nothing of one another's existence. That led to the colonial period, which involved even more extensive contact between different societies, the ultimate consequence being a number of multi-racial societies, of which there had previously been almost none.

The second is the mid-15th-century development of the printing press by Johannes Gutenberg. This becomes a major factor in our story for many reasons. The printing press brought about the spread of literacy. This meant that knowledge about faraway lands and peoples would become increasingly available by means of books, pamphlets, newspapers, and magazines. It also meant that, with a much-enlarged reading public, ideas could spread widely and comparatively rapidly. This spread of ideas and information meant that the scale and impact of public opinion would be greatly increased. And that, in turn, meant that ideas concerning the rights and wrongs of human behavior could become a far more powerful force in human affairs.

The third factor is the fragmentation of European Christianity resulting from the corruption of the Catholic Church, which had reached its height at the time of the papacy of Alexander VI (1492–1503). Protestantism proper, with its ally the soon-to-be-independent Anglican Church, freed northern Europe to go its own way, and as a result the center of gravity of European thought and science began to move northward. (As we'll see, Protestantism was another significant factor in the development of literacy.) It was those northern European states that would be most prominent in the development of modern science and technology, and more generally of modernity itself. And it was in that context that the changed attitudes towards other peoples would develop.

When we begin at 1500, the first question we should ask might seem to be: what attitudes did people of that time have toward cultures other than their own? But this question reminds me of the exclamation by Goethe's Faust: "Hier stock' ich schon!" ("I am pulled up short already!") The question can't be answered until we've first looked at another that it depends on: what did the average member of any one society really know about other cultures at this time? Their opinions can only have been based on what they knew—so how much did they know? And the answer to that question is perfectly clear: they knew next to nothing.

Why was this? Think about where we get our knowledge of other cultures today. In the modern era we can draw on knowledge from a great many sources: from travel that can take us half-way across the globe in a few hours; from books, magazines, and newspapers; from radio, TV, film, and the internet. Drawing on all these resources, today we can easily learn a great deal about societies and peoples other than our own. But in the world of 1500, not one of those resources was available.

At what point in history did these advantages that we now have appear? First, travel: it took the invention of the steam engine to give us travel by rail. The first fully functional steam engine was invented by British mechanical engineer James Watt only in the late 18th century, and the first railroad using steam power was built by Richard Trevithick, another British engineer, but not until the early 19th century. The steam engine also gave us fast ships: in 1838 the SS Great Western, designed by yet another British engineer—Isambard Kingdom Brunel—crossed the Atlantic in fifteen days, less than half the time taken by sailing ships. The internal combustion engine gave us automobiles and trucks, but it was not invented until 1860, and the first motor vehicles using it didn't come off the production line until the 1880s.

In 1500, therefore, transport over land was fastest by horse, with or without a carriage, and even that was only available to a relatively small, well-to-do segment of the community. For most, travel occurred by foot, which meant that they probably never went further than about thirty miles from where they were born. Given that limitation, the great majority of people never saw cultures other than their own, nor even an individual from another culture, except under highly unpleasant circumstances— namely, warfare.

Radio, films, television, internet? Again, these are all resources that lay in the very distant future for the people of 1500. Radio and film begin around the turn of the 19th to 20th centuries and television toward the middle of the 20th century. Guglielmo Marconi, who was born in Italy but was fluent in English and worked in England, sent the first radio transmissions in the last few years of the 19th century. The first silent film showing was in 1895 in Paris. The Scottish engineer John Logie Baird demonstrated the first television set in 1927. All of these things were hundreds of years in the future for the peoples of 1500.

As to print media: very few people in 1500 had access to information from books and other printed materials. To be sure, Gutenberg's press was invented in 1455, but books manufactured by printing presses with movable type were at first expensive. They would not be cheap enough for the average person to buy for several hundred years. And in any case, there were initially not many of them. In 1500, few people were literate. Before books, pamphlets, and magazines could efficiently spread knowledge of foreign cultures, therefore, they would not only have to become cheaper and more plentiful, but people would also have to learn to read them. In 1500, literacy was still restricted to monks, scribes, and relatively few people with money and power. The significant exceptions to this generalization were the Jews, who as early as the 1st century A.D. taught their children to read the Torah. For all other groups the spread of literacy was slow, though eventually—in the 18th and 19th centuries— it would become crucial for the spread of modern ideas and attitudes concerning other peoples.

In the modern world, yet another common source of knowledge of foreign cultures is personal experience: we know, work with, and are related by marriage to all kinds of people who are different from ourselves in race and/or national origin. We have come to rely on them, to respect them, and to admire many of the public figures among them. But for the most part this kind of personal knowledge wasn't available to people living in 1500, the exception again being warfare, a special case that did nothing whatsoever to foster good-will between different cultures.

Some truths are so obvious that we easily miss their force and meaning. If we say that in 1500 almost all Europeans were in Europe, almost all Africans were in Africa, almost all Chinese were in China, and so on, that may sound almost tautological, but it's still an important fact of history. Until disturbed, the status quo on the globe was that peoples who had adapted physically to a certain kind of terrain and climate, and consequently shared certain characteristics that had resulted from that adaptation, would mostly be found in the place where those characteristics developed. There is no place on earth where for thousands of years Africans developed their characteristic features side by side with people who developed in a completely different way—say, with much paler skins. Peoples almost always remained where they had adapted to their environment, and as a result population groups in contiguous places would have looked rather similar to each other, and noticeably different to people who lived in greatly different environments.

Before 1500, this was, for the most part, the status quo. If peoples moved at all, they tended to move to areas similar in climate to the ones they left. Some European populations had moved, but they moved within Europe. Polynesians had learned to travel long distances on the seas, but a typical result would find Tahitians winding up in Hawaii. Moreover, this kind of large migration was a once-in-a-millennium, whole-population shift, bearing little similarity to the reality of many regions today, in which different racial groups interact regularly and intimately. Prior to 1500, the Mediterranean region was probably, more than anywhere else, where cultures had mixed with, clashed with, traded with, and influenced one another. Islands on the Mediterranean—Crete, for example—were close to three different continents: Europe, Asia, and Africa. Crossing the Mediterranean from one continent to another by ship was relatively easy and efficient. Yet even here, warfare was still the major cause of contact between cultures.

Today, some people in certain predominantly White societies have started to feel guilty that everyone seems to look the same. They have come to feel that a mono-racial society is somehow morally reprehensible. Scandinavians, especially, appear to believe that it is shameful for a population to be all-White, and they have therefore hastily imported non-Europeans into their country. France and Germany have acted similarly, going out of their way to import non-European populations in a fit of politically correct virtue-signaling. This artificial, ill-considered scheme has only resulted in Sweden's now having crime rates that it has never seen before, and France's having enclaves (the banlieues) that Frenchmen—even French police—dare not enter. In Germany the influx of immigration led to a political crisis that became so severe, it forced a reversal in policy. Those who legislated these population shifts seem not to have recognized that the resulting society would include not only many races, but also many cultures. And those cultures might in some ways prove incompatible.

What originally led to this impasse was an irrational moral panic. White skin tones developed in northern areas of the globe, where there was much less sunshine than elsewhere. Why should people whose skin color was an adaptation to those conditions feel bad about not living among peoples whose traits developed differently, in different climates, thousands of miles to the south? If those southern peoples had lived together with Scandinavians in Scandinavia for an appreciable length of time, they too would have become as pale as the Scandinavians. There is no valid reason to feel guilty about something that came into being through a normal process of adaptation. Sweden was responding hastily and thoughtlessly to woke imperatives, but one might note that the people they were so desperate to import never shared their bien-pensant attitudes. In the places that they came from, the prevailing attitude towards foreigners was the exact opposite—namely, that only people who looked like themselves belonged where they lived. That's now the prevailing attitude in Zimbabwe, for example.

In 1500, then, most people knew very little about cultures other than their own. In a world where, by modern standards, travel was extremely primitive, an almost complete ignorance of other peoples prevailed. What attitudes they had formed about those peoples can therefore only have been based on ignorance, and ignorance almost guaranteed that they would be apprehensive towards, if not outright fearful of, other peoples. They were unlikely to come naturally to the conclusion that people about which they knew nothing were probably splendid fellows.

This tendency to fear the unknown was not an unreasonable reaction. On most occasions when different peoples met each other, the result would have been highly unpleasant. Wars between neighboring peoples were commonplace. Even in the absence of outright tribal war, people still lived in fear of marauding foreigners. A relaxed harmony between adjacent nationalities or tribes rarely existed anywhere.

As a general rule, therefore, in earlier times different cultures didn't admire one another, but on the contrary were suspicious and hostile, always fearing conflict. People saw safety in the protection afforded by people like themselves, and they saw only danger in contact with people beyond their own tribe. The rule in 1500 was not *gens una sumus*, but the very different "my brother and I against my cousin; my cousin and I against the stranger." The less like you someone was, the more dangerous he was likely to be. People worried only about the well-being of their own tribe, and they left it to other tribes to look out for theirs. Everyone assumed that the tribe they belonged to had quite enough to do looking out for itself. What was good for one's own people trumped what was good for other peoples, hands down.

Today's radical academic would probably describe this attitude as racist, but it wasn't. It was, rather, a necessary prudence, given the conditions of 1500. Not to be wary of neighboring peoples, and not to be prepared for conflict, would have been negligent. Nobody would even have understood what you meant if, in 1500, you had accused them of racism.

This state of affairs persisted long after 1500. Accordingly, to call the American colonialists and Founders racist (the verdict of The 1619 Project's Nikole Hannah-Jones) makes no sense whatever. In a dangerous world, they, like everyone else, attended first to their own group's survival. They knew perfectly well that that survival could only be assured by hard work, intelligent management, and good luck. Like everyone else, they left to other groups the concern for their survival, and they could be confident that those other groups felt much the same way.

Wars were fought in these times over all kinds of things: food and hunting grounds, women, territory, power. Sometimes it almost seemed as if wars were fought for war's sake, as if war was simply the way of life.

But there was always one thing that made war especially likely: the need to ensure a reliable supply of food. Modern people can scarcely imagine how powerful that sort of anxiety was. Without trucking, food could only be sourced locally, and without electrical refrigeration, many foods would not keep for long. Especially in northern climates, stocking enough food to last through winter required extremely careful planning. Many foods could be stored given the right conditions, provided that preservatives such as salt were available. Further, game and livestock could be killed for fresh meat, cows could provide milk, and chickens could provide eggs. But these various means of ensuring food throughout the winter could be annihilated unless you could defend your land, your supplies, and your animals against invaders. If you couldn't, you'd starve. (The invaders were probably close to starving too.) You might have just as well been killed in combat. Food planning thus took prudence, intelligence, and hard work—but above all security. Outsiders were a constant threat: they could take everything from you and leave you helpless. Who could afford to live by *gens una sumus* in conditions like these?

The challenges were somewhat different for small tribal communities than they were for larger nation-states, though never less than serious for both. Among the former, tribal warfare was almost the norm. Sometimes this consisted in one tribe opportunistically raiding another tribe's food or women, but at other times more lasting claims were made. The invaders might want your land—your hunting grounds. In such cases the war might be fought to the extinction of one side, for the simple reason that this was the only way to settle things once and for all. War to extinction happened all over the globe, and the practice has not yet completely disappeared, even today.

When Shaka, the Zulu chieftain, was building an empire in 19th-century Africa, his armies slaughtered entire populations—men, women, and children—whenever they encountered resistance. Robert Edgerton reports the horrific fact that "it took no longer than ninety minutes for the Zulu army to destroy the Ndwandwe, leaving some 40,000 men, women, and children dead in the field."[1] Brotherly love between different peoples was never likely in conditions such as these.

Warfare between small tribes could be just as brutal. Edgerton found that warfare among local tribes was ferocious and incessant in places as far apart as Papua, Tasmania, and North America—even among the Inuit of the far north. The Kaiadilt of Australia "were close to extinction as a result of their raids to capture women."[2] In these kinds of tribal settings, people who were captured in battle could be enslaved, tortured, even eaten. And primitive societies were rarely sexually enlightened. Being stronger, men abused women at their whim. Just one of the many powerful reasons to fear neighboring tribes was that your women might be brutalized in consequence of warfare initiated by those tribes.

Across the globe, raids on neighboring tribes for food, valuables, women, or land were simply a way of life. The idea that particular tribes always acknowledged other tribes as the rightful owners of certain lands is a fiction devised by modern radicals bent on discrediting European colonialism. The case of the celebrated last survivor of the Yahi tribe—Ishi—illustrates the point. The decline of the Yahi began when they were displaced by the much larger Wintu tribe. The Yahi fled to more mountainous but less productive land, where their numbers began to dwindle.[3]

Tribes could certainly cooperate from time to time, but that usually happened only when they were ganging up on another tribe that they all hated. The Pequot War of 1636–38 is a case in point. The Pequot systematically extended their territory at the expense of several other tribes, attacking and killing any who stood in their way. Their victims included Europeans settlers, but they terrorized all their neighboring tribes, indigenous and non-indigenous alike. Eventually, this reign of terror caused several tribes to band together to defeat the Pequot, who were all but exterminated as a result. European settlers are sometimes accused of "massacring" them, but the settlers were only one of the groups that banded together to deal with the lethal menace of the Pequot. Where the extermination of the Pequot is concerned, it can justifiably be said that the tribes that banded together to kill them acted in self-defense. A similar case is that of the six tribes that joined together in their hatred of the Tonkawa Indians' enthusiastic cannibalism. Even the Spanish conquistador Hernán Cortés found allies in tribes who hated the Aztecs, fear of cannibalism again being the factor which united those tribes with each other and with him.[4] This cooperation was surely inspired not by love of one's fellow man, but rather by hatred of a particular enemy group.

It's easy to see that, in these conditions, identification with one's own tribe would naturally be intense: this community was the only reliable protection that tribal people had. There is a recurring phenomenon that shows how strongly peoples in earlier times felt about this allegiance. "Deutsch" is the word that modern-day Germans use to refer to themselves, but historically it derives from "diota," an older word, occurring in the earliest recorded stage of the German language, meaning "the people." One sees similar etymologies in many other cultures and places. The Navajo, for instance, call themselves Diné, which also means, simply, "the people." Robert Edgerton comments on this practice: "People in many societies refer to themselves as 'the people' and regard all others as alien and repellent, if not downright subhuman." Edgerton continues: "It is not uncommon for a population to think of itself as the best people on earth, even the only people on earth...."[5] Again, this cultural tendency can't be regarded as a form of racism. Instead, it reflects a sense that the only real protection one could rely on was one's own people. In these conditions, *gens una sumus* would have been a suicidal policy.

Early Europe certainly saw plenty of opportunistic tribal warfare. Viking raids on coastal Europe, for instance, were constant and terrifying. But before we judge the Vikings as amoral thieves and murderers, we must always remember that the conditions of life at these times were precarious, and that everyone's primary goal was to ensure the survival of one's own people—if need be, at the expense of another tribe's survival. Adverse moral judgments made much later completely miss the insecurity of life in earlier times.

As large nation-states began to develop in Europe, the universal hostility to strangers and neighbors from other cultures began to take on a different shape, because in this changing situation the dangers took a different form. Nation-states were much larger units than tribes, and, accordingly, seeking security against invasion or marauding became a rather different matter than it had been. Citizens of nation-states certainly had one advantage over tribal members: the people in neighboring villages or towns were no longer threats to one another, as they were in tribal societies, because they had become a single people. Under the broader nation-state, one felt kinship with neighboring villagers, seeing them as fellow countrymen. But in quelling hostilities between immediate neighbors, nation-states acquired another problem that was in some ways worse. For every single European nation-state eyed its neighboring nation-states nervously, fearing invasion.

Nation-states were formed by slow accumulations of territory, as one people conquered and absorbed another. A general principle soon emerged: bigger is better. Larger states were obviously more secure than smaller ones. If a nation could gain territory and people by annexing a smaller neighbor, it would correspondingly become somewhat more powerful and thus safer against invasion. Even today, Russia has still not abandoned this age-old attitude, and it's telling that almost all other European countries regard Russia's invasion of Ukraine as a throwback to a past that nobody now wants to return to.

In 1500 and long after, the major European nations were still trying to make themselves more secure by expanding their borders. Spain absorbed the Netherlands; England hoped to conquer a good part of France; Austria acquired Eastern European territories; Sweden occupied parts of Finland, Lithuania, Russia, and Germany. Russia was always bent on maximal conquest, and it expanded a good deal under Peter the Great. In the 17th century, everyone lived in fear of the expansionary plans of the megalomaniac French king, Louis XIV.

Some of these acquisitions stuck, but most didn't. One result of this constant jostling of power and territory was that European nations became obsessed with the "balance of power" in Europe. This more abstract understanding of national security began to replace or at least supplement the principle of "bigger is better." In this way of thinking, a nation could attain the same benefits of military expansion, but through the cheaper and more bloodless method of forming alliances with other nation-states. A bloc of allied states could withstand aggression from a state that was larger than any single country in the bloc. (NATO is a modern example of the same principle.) That made it possible for a state to achieve greater security without being absorbed by another state, thus preserving its national identity.

Sometimes this balance-of-power diplomacy worked as intended, and sometimes it didn't. The Austrian diplomat Klemens von Metternich was a major player in balance-of-power diplomacy in Europe in the first half of the 19th century. Following the defeat of Napoleon in 1815, he (and others who were similarly minded) decided to guard against a revival of French power by giving the Rhineland and Westphalia to Prussia, thus creating a strong anti-French force to guard France's eastern boundary. But Metternich had only solved one balance-of-power problem by creating another, which, in the long run, turned out much worse for Austria. A strengthened Prussia meant that the eventual unification of the numerous German-speaking states of Europe in 1871 into what we now call Germany was led by Prussia, not Austria. Worse, it *excluded* Austria. In the long run, what Metternich had achieved by his maneuvering to contain France was the eventual end of the Austrian Empire, and its decline to the status of a minor European country. Without Metternich's scheming it might instead have been the center and headquarters of a different kind of newly united German-speaking nation. In this case, balance-of-power diplomacy turned out to be almost as hazardous as warfare itself.

But even balance-of-power diplomacy could not stop countries from eyeing their neighbors nervously, nor could it remove the fear of invasion that was always present among ordinary people. Animosity between neighboring powers remained just as strong in Europe as it was between tribes of less developed societies. The big difference was that when primitive tribes attacked each other, the wars involved the whole tribal populations, but where nation-states were concerned, the fighting was done by professional soldiers. One might think that this would limit the damage to a small segment of a country's population, but it didn't. In fact, it made things worse—much worse—for all the people of the countries involved.

Invading armies made the problem of food security many times more dangerous. An army—whether invading or defending—fed itself by grabbing whatever food was available in the immediate vicinity. Soldiers looked for the food stores of civilians, and if they found yours, you'd starve, because your provisions, especially those you had set aside for the winter, would be gone. The armies would not only take your stored food; they might also butcher your livestock, depriving you of your steady, year-round provisions of eggs and milk. All of this meant that war between the armies of nation-states was a terrifying prospect for civilians. The worst of it was, it didn't matter whether you were overrun by your own troops or invading armies—both would plunder your food stores and leave you to starve. And when large numbers of soldiers moved from one territory to another, they were also likely to spread infectious diseases.

The most extreme example of this kind of devastation was the European Thirty Years' War of 1618–1648. Peter Wilson estimates that deaths of soldiers during the war were about 450,000, but civilian deaths were well over ten times that figure.[6] The verdict of the historian Hajo Holborn is that "Germany lost her position as the most populous country in Europe, her population of about 20 million having dropped to between 12 and 13 million."[7] Holborn made this estimate already in 1964, and it appears to have remained the consensus view in historical work done since then. The much more modern (2009) estimate of Wilson was still that there were 8 million deaths during the war.[8] These millions of civilians died of starvation and disease—the latter deaths were of course related to the former. Some areas saw their populations drop by as much as 60 percent. Over its thirty-year duration, the war was indescribably complex, involving a succession of different coalitions, reversals of fortune, and a constantly changing list of warring nations. But there's no need to grasp all the ups and downs of the war to understand in general how and why it was so destructive.

The Thirty Years' War began when a newly elected ruler of two small states (Styria and Bohemia) imposed Catholicism on one of them and seemed likely to do the same with the other. This upset Protestants, and fighting began. Over the next thirty years, a long list of other European states joined in, one by one. New states sometimes joined for religious reasons, but as time went on, increasingly they entered the fray to keep either side from accumulating too much power. This led to ever-changing coalitions. The shape, purpose, and extent of warfare constantly shifted, and the battle lines therefore changed constantly, so that the same area could be first overrun by one army, then by another as the first retreated, then yet again as an initial aggressor, newly reinforced, advanced once more. In this way the battle line kept going backwards and forwards, with the same area being devastated time after time—for all of thirty years. As one side advanced it took all the food it could find, and as it was pushed back by a newly strengthened opposition it would retreat over the same area, grabbing any food that remained. Yet another plundering took place as the advancing army reached that same area, and this scavenging for any last vestige of food might be repeated yet again. The Thirty Years' War was an extreme case, but warfare between European nation-states at this stage of history generally shattered civilian populations.

The year 1500 was, as it happens, a particularly frightening one, as far as Europeans were concerned. The Ottoman Empire was in the process of becoming one of the largest empires the world has ever seen, conquering one country after another in the area surrounding the Mediterranean, and reaching further into southern Europe. Before they were stopped at the gates of Vienna in 1683, the Ottomans had conquered a huge territory, eventually controlling what is now Bulgaria, Hungary, Albania, Serbia, Croatia, Slovenia, Bosnia, Greece, Macedonia, Crimea, Armenia, Azerbaijan, Romania, Egypt, Tunisia, Algeria, Moldova, Lebanon, Iraq, Israel, Saudi Arabia, Libya, and Lebanon. The Ottomans enslaved Europeans in large numbers and treated them brutally. They made concubines of women. Their biggest territorial gains were made around the year 1500. The prospect of the Ottomans pressing further into Europe must have been extraordinarily frightening to ordinary people.

It's not hard to imagine how wars like these would have affected how people thought about different cultures at this time. At the forefront of their minds was not brotherly love for their fellow man, but rather an all-consuming fear. For most, the calculus was very simple: people from other cultures means danger—terrible danger. Tribal solidarity and inter-tribal hostility are inevitably the norm where invaders are a constant source of anxiety. In a highly dangerous world, people could only expect protection from their own kind—from people like themselves, people of the same language and culture—and from nobody else. Born into the same historical conditions, our present-day woke moralists would have seen the world in very much the same way: they would have followed their instincts for survival. In these conditions, *gens una sumus* was an idea that was a long way off in the distant future. To call people of this era "racist" would be the height of historical ignorance—and stupidity. To take them to task for their "orientalism"—that is, for developing caricatured notions of Turks—would be just as foolish.[9] The fears that ordinary people had were based on very real threats, endangering nothing less than their life and liberty. Only in the fevered imaginations of pampered scholars, living hundreds of years later in an infinitely safer era, could those fears be interpreted as grievous moral failings. Nor is there any need to excuse or explain away the actions and thoughts of those people as demonstrating the limitations of their times. Their actions were rational and necessary. *Gens una sumus* is a modern luxury, made possible only by living conditions that are far more secure than those of 1500.

Even today, many of the peoples of the world are still more inclined to the older ideology of "my brother and I against my cousin; my cousin and I against the stranger," than they are to *gens una sumus*. If radical scholars were really concerned about racist lapses from our great modern guiding principle of *gens una sumus*, they wouldn't look to a distant past where that principle could never have prevailed. They could instead easily find examples of whole societies where that "racist" ideology is still alive and well—in the Middle East, for example. But instead of looking for racism where it is blatant and abundant, they seek it in the one place where it's getting hard to find—in their own society. That discrepancy tells us what really motivates these scholars: not the correction of racism, but a radical determination to condemn the society that they themselves are part of.

It's hard for modern people to imagine the insecurity of life in 1500, and how that must have affected the attitudes of people who lived then. Average life expectancy even of Europeans was in the thirties, less than half what it is today.[10] Social safety nets didn't exist: social security and welfare legislation were far off in the future. Infant mortality rates were horrendous, and they remained so for years to come. In the late 17th century, Britain's Queen Anne had seventeen pregnancies which resulted in only ten births, and not one of those children survived to maturity. Competent medical care was almost non-existent. For most people, banking didn't exist. Law and order as we understand it barely existed, so that protection from thieves was minimal and travel on public highways was dangerous. In conditions like these, people were busy enough securing their own survival. It would take a far greater degree of security before the average person could start to worry about the welfare of other societies.

The change in attitudes to other peoples that has developed between 1500 and modern times has been profound, and it is one of the greatest gifts that modernity has given us. But the change happened slowly, and it certainly didn't just happen on its own. Human beings didn't suddenly wake up and become more well-intentioned toward each other; they didn't spontaneously become nicer people. On the contrary, the change occurred because of certain specific historical events. Those events happened because specific groups of people made them happen. The rest of this book is devoted to tracing just what those events were and how they unfolded.

As we look at the pivotal stages in history from 1500 to the present day, there are three principles that must always be kept in mind. First, the crucial changes that took place, leading us towards *gens una sumus*, must be measured against the conditions of 1500, not those of today. Modern scholars generally do exactly the opposite: they look at these transitional developments and measure them against contemporary moral standards, finding them wanting, even immoral. That's a political activist's way of looking at history, not a historian's.

A clearer way of illustrating this point is to think about a glass whose state can be described in one of two ways: we can call it either half-full or half-empty, even though both refer to the same condition. Where the principle of *gens una sumus* is concerned, the glass was empty in 1500. It then begins to fill up gradually, leading us to today, when it is nearly full, though not completely so. The right way to describe that glass in 1800 is that it is approaching half full: that is, it has made very significant progress since being empty in 1500. But when modern radicals complain about the racism of people in and around 1800, they are effectively calling the glass half empty, because they are only thinking about how it contained so much less than it does today.

The second point is a corollary of the first. Activist modern scholars speak as if their modern ethos were the natural one, from which it follows that any action that doesn't meet the standard of *gens una sumus*, in any historical period, must represent moral failure. But history teaches us something quite different: it's the ethos of 1500 that is the default condition of history, while the present-day commitment to *gens una sumus* is something that was learned over many centuries. It had to be created by thinkers who formulated it and then argued for it, eventually persuading a steadily growing number of people of its desirability. The history of the period from 1500 onward is one of the deliberate creation and slow adoption of attitudes that had to displace a completely different set of deeply ingrained attitudes. Anyone who doubts which attitudes are the more natural need only consider how those older, more tribal attitudes reassert themselves today whenever they have the chance to do so.

The third point is that when we make moral judgments of individuals of earlier times, it's not enough simply to measure them against a historical development that begins in 1500 and ends at the present day. We must also look at how they stood within the context of their own time. Did they just reflect the mores of their time—were they just like everyone else of that period? Or were they instead at the forefront of change, leaders in the move toward *gens una sumus*? As we'll see, the very same historical figures who today are frequently criticized for attitudes that don't meet today's standards, often turn out to have been exceptional leaders in developing those modern standards.

The people who were central to the creation of modern attitudes are, in fact, the heroes of our story. They were the ones who led us beyond the conditions of the year 1500. Radical modern scholars think that if those people were less enlightened than we are now, they can be dismissed as racists. This is a failure of historical understanding—a failure that leads, for example, to the foolishness of pulling down statues of the very people who developed the ideas that these confused virtue-signalers now embrace.

Chapter Two: The Age of Discovery

AS WE'VE SEEN, the way in which one group of people looked at another in 1500 AD was starkly different from what it is today. People trusted their own kind and were apprehensive about everyone else—and they had good reasons for being so. They found safety in people they knew, and they saw danger in those they didn't. How, then, did we get from that attitude to *gens una sumus*, the reigning philosophy of today? How did that happen? The first key development that led us towards the modern ideology takes such a circuitous route that, though crucial for what was eventually to follow, it made things, if anything, somewhat worse in the short term. In this first stage, known as the Age of Discovery, Europeans met peoples who were culturally far less developed than themselves. This was hardly likely to be a good basis for a sense of oneness with them.

In our own time, we frequently hear objections to the name given long ago to this era: the Age of Discovery. That's a misnomer, it's said, because the lands that Europeans discovered at that time had already been discovered by the people who lived there. This objection completely misses the point. The Age of Discovery changed the course of world history. What's important is not what we call it, but how it changed the world.

To understand how fundamental the change was, we must first focus on the characteristic feature of the pre-discovery world that was about to be changed forever. In the 15th century, the largest part of the world formed a relatively contiguous land mass in which each country was bordered by or was within easy reach of one or more other countries. Every country in this series of adjacent countries was—however vaguely —known to exist by every other in the chain. We'll call this the "known world," a broader idea than the commonly used term "old world," which is generally taken to refer only to Europe. The opposite of the known world is not the "new world"—which generally refers only to the Americas—but the "unknown world."

The known world included all of Europe and Asia, and part of North Africa. At least some Europeans not only understood the extent of European countries, but also knew of the existence of Asian and Mediterranean cultures. Africa was a special case: its northern area belonged to the known world even in ancient times, but the Sahara Desert was a barrier that was almost as effective as the Atlantic Ocean. As a result, sub-Saharan cultures were virtually as isolated from the rest of the world as the Americas were.

The known world consisted, therefore, of a very large number of peoples. All manner of innovations—for example, agriculture, metallurgy, and gunpowder—had been able, however slowly, to spread along this great chain of cultures. Diseases could travel along the chain too, and did so over thousands of years, which meant that the known world was in effect one large pool of adapted immunities. But in addition to this chain of cultures that knew of and continually influenced one another, the world also contained cultures that were isolated not just from the known world, but from most of the other cultures not part of the known world. They all shared one important limitation: since they were not part of the linked system of the known world, the innovations that had emerged from time to time in different places in that world and then spread throughout it had never reached them.

It's true that in the Americas of 1500 there were many tribes that, while isolated both from the known world and from hitherto unknown cultures in other parts of the world, were nonetheless in touch with those adjacent to them. But even here, innovations do not seem to have traveled throughout the cultures of the Americas as they had done in the known world. For example, some tribes had agriculture, and some didn't. Some had impressive buildings, but most didn't. Many were in a technological Stone Age, yet a few practiced metallurgy. There are probably three reasons why innovations didn't spread throughout the Americas as they had in the known world. First is the fact that, here, transportation was even more primitive than it was in the known world. Before the Age of Discovery, horses were unknown in the Americas and arrived there only when Hernán Cortés released them on the mainland in the 16th century. Land travel therefore took place only by foot. The second is a matter of relative population density. Before the arrival of Europeans there were relatively few people per square mile in the Americas—certainly far fewer than was the case in the known world. Third is that anatomically modern humans had been in Europe for a much longer period of time than they had been in the Americas—probably something like three times as long.

The cultures that had been largely isolated from the known world and from each other until the Age of Discovery included, in addition to those of the Americas, those of Australia, New Zealand, sub-Saharan Africa, and many islands or island chains. By that time major technological innovations such as the wheel, agriculture, construction with stone, metallurgy, writing, and gunpowder had spread across the known world, but they had not reached most parts of the isolated, unknown world.

The most important result of the Age of Discovery was that those previously isolated peoples finally began to enter the system of the known world. Accordingly, they would soon benefit from its innovations. Whatever the detractors of the discoverers may say, this was a development of profound importance. It would turn out to be the first stage of a long process that would eventually overcome what had been the state of the world up to that time, one in which different peoples clung to their own, fearing and mistrusting others.

Today we are prone to assume that many parts of the world are quite naturally multi-ethnic—but they aren't, as a quick look at history shows. Singapore is the example that most readily springs to mind: it's now a place where Malays, Chinese, Indians, and people of other races live side-by-side. That condition is now so settled that it seems it must have been so forever. But the truth is that this mix has only existed during the last few hundred years. It was the Age of Discovery that set the world moving toward the multi-racial societies that now include the United States, Canada, Australia, New Zealand, South Africa, Great Britain, and many others.

Without the Age of Discovery or a possible later episode of the kind, the peoples of the world would largely have remained where they first developed through their adaptation to a particular environment. The different races would still be mostly separated from each other, and they would exist at different stages of civilizational development. According to our modern standards, that would seem like an apartheid world. It was because of the Age of Discovery that people began to meet other cultures and races as never before. And they met those peoples not just as individual traders or travelers, but in serious numbers. Moreover, they weren't just mixing with neighboring populations, but with populations who lived a long way away from their own homes, and in parts of the world that had been previously unknown to them.

To return to a point made in the previous chapter: different races adapted differently to different environments in different parts of the world. Their original state could therefore only have been one of separateness from each other, because their characteristic features arose in the distinct environments in which they developed. That could not have been otherwise. Only the great distances that the seafarers of the Age of Discovery were able to travel brought peoples of very different races and starkly unequal stages of development into contact with each other, and so made a future of multi-racial societies possible. This was, therefore, the beginning of the mixing of different population groups that is now commonplace in our modern world.

This is not to say that tribes or peoples had never changed locations before, or that some had not traveled quite large distances. Even within the Americas, for example, around 1400 AD, some tribes of the Athabascan language family of western North America split off from the main group that was located mostly in what is now western Canada, migrating hundreds of miles south to what is now Arizona and New Mexico. But they have stayed there ever since; this, again, was a once-in-a-millennium population shift, not a regular intermingling of peoples in the course of their daily lives. In the known world, the largest known movement of peoples had been the great "Völkerwanderung" (migration of the peoples) of the 5th century AD, when the westward invasion of Attila the Hun triggered the chaotic flight of Europeans who were in his path. Countless tribes would wind up settling hundreds of miles from where they had been. But when these tribes settled down again, they too remained where they ended up, and they are still there today. No serious mixing of tribes who were at greatly different levels of development had taken place, and in all these cases their descendants, who became the people of 1500 AD, typically remained in the place where they were born.

The same was true of the movement of the Norsemen, for example into France and then England in the Middle Ages. The Normans (the shortened form of their name following their conquest of what became Normandy) conquered England after they had taken France, but this was no more than a reshuffling of different Germanic tribes: the Saxons, Angles, Frisians, and Norsemen were all closely related. In all of this, no mixing of fundamentally different peoples took place.

The Age of Discovery was something completely different: it was no longer a question of peoples simply bumping into and displacing or conquering their next-door neighbors. Now a group of nations set out to explore the entire globe, traveling huge distances, reaching places that had been unknown, and encountering peoples who didn't look at all like themselves—peoples who had developed in completely different environments and therefore in completely different ways. For the first time, substantial numbers of Europeans met peoples from beyond the known world in their original setting. This contact with the unknown world would eventually lead to a completely different European attitude toward foreign cultures: *gens una sumus* would first become reality in the multi-racial societies that arose as a result of the Age of Discovery.

It was no accident that Europeans set this ball rolling. The seafaring nations of Europe were always most likely to be the major force that eventually undertook to unify the world. By this time they had superior ocean-going ships, together with magnetic compasses for navigation. The most celebrated date associated with the onset of the Age of Discovery is 1492, the year of Christopher Columbus's voyage across the Atlantic—though by then the Portuguese had already begun their own voyages of discovery. By 1500 the more northerly nations of Europe— Britain, Holland, France, and Belgium—had joined in, and already their increasing prosperity began to tilt the race to discover in their favor.

What motivated these Europeans? That is a much discussed and disputed question. There is no simple answer, but many different factors can readily be discerned. There was certainly an expectation of economic benefits, but it would be a mistake to assume that greed was the only or even the dominant catalyst. There was also pure curiosity: who and what was beyond the known world? Probably more important than both of these motives, however, was a desire that goes back to the reigning principle of security in that era: bigger is better, because stronger and safer. When Portugal and Spain expanded into newly discovered territories, the rest of Europe naturally became uneasy about the growing power of these two states. The response of the seafaring nations of northern Europe was inevitable—if they did nothing, they'd be more vulnerable to the increasing power of their southern neighbors. If the British didn't immediately set out to find newly discovered lands of their own, the Dutch, Spanish, Portuguese, and French would.

At this stage, virtually every European nation feared the power of its neighbors, and anything that was likely to increase the power of one's enemies was bound to be disturbing. If one nation stood by while others strengthened themselves with colonies, that nation would become less secure. The proof of this pudding is in the eating: there can be little doubt that Britain's enviable record of almost a thousand years without invasion by another country (from 1066 to the present) owes a great deal to its empire and to the navy that serviced it. A small island with a limited population was able to ward off all invaders—even during the post-1500 period, when almost every other European power had to fight wars on its own soil many times over. From a strategic point of view, England's strengthening itself with an empire was elementary prudence given the state of the world both in 1500 and in the centuries to come.

The most important motive animating all of these seafaring nations was therefore the same: if any one nation-state stayed the same size while its neighbors grew larger and more powerful, it would become more vulnerable. The rational response was to make sure that you grew in power as others did. Nobody doubted that bigger was safer, nor did anyone think that there was a convincing moral objection to that way of thinking. Nobody lived yet by the ethos of *gens una sumus*, and nobody had qualms about becoming stronger by means of empire if that meant a lower risk of being brutalized by other peoples. A well-known British anthem is based on that very idea: "Rule, Britannia! Britannia rules the waves, Britons never, never, never, shall be slaves." And they never were since Roman times. Once more, racism had nothing to do with this, because anyone who lived at the time of the Age of Discovery would have seen the world in the same way. It would have been folly not to.

The most interesting instance of empires expanding into new territories mainly because they were anxious that other nations might get there first was in Africa. Colonization came quite late in Africa, and not much happened there in the way of European involvement before the mid-19th century. The historian Niall Ferguson ventured the opinion that ". . . it is impossible to understand the scramble for Africa without seeing that it had its antecedents in the perennial power struggle between the great powers to maintain—or overthrow—the balance of power between them in Europe or the Near East."[1]

When it came to empire at these times in history, the only consideration that really mattered was not a moral but a practical one: feasibility. All peoples built empires if they could. Living in peace was everyone's wish, but that meant being maximally protected from other nations. The history of the world up to 1500 leaves no room for doubt about the force of this practical motive, because it had been so for all recorded time.

Wikipedia lists a total of 290 empires throughout human history, but the entry also cautions that this is an incomplete list.[2] Empires existed in all eras, from the Persians, the Romans, and the Hittites in antiquity, through the British Empire beginning in the 17th century, right up to the Soviet and Japanese empires of the 20th century. They existed on every habitable continent of the earth: the Aztecs of North America; the Incas of South America; the Austrian, French, Portuguese, Dutch, and German empires of Europe; the massive Japanese, Russian, Chinese, and Mongolian empires of Asia; the African empires of the Zulus, Ashanti, Mali, and Songhai; and the early Muslim empire of the Abuyyid, as well as the later Ottoman, Safavid, and Mughal empires. A curious fact is that overrunning an adjacent country appears less likely to be described by historians as "imperialism" than is conquering a distant land reached only by sea. Russia has long held large territories peopled by non-Russian speakers, but it is not often accused of imperialism. The present Russian Federation is certainly the largest remaining empire on earth.

Though empires have existed at all times and in all places of human history, and among all races and religions, radical historians now want to ignore the hundreds of non-Western empires that have existed throughout history so that they can frame empire as a uniquely European, and thus White supremacist, phenomenon. That is either ignorant or dishonest. Until quite recently, any group of people that were able to conquer other people and territory did so, because that was a rational response to a dangerous world.

There are certainly many differences in how different empires were run, and how empires treated the peoples that they controlled. There is, however, one crucial respect in which the British Empire can be distinguished from all others. That empire ended not by external compulsion (that is, by military defeat), but by the voluntary action of its own people. It was, for this very reason, the last of the great empires and as such an important factor in the spread of the philosophy of *gens una sumus*.

In the modern era, when that philosophy has finally become the prevailing, or (to be more accurate) the official ethos of the world, it is perfectly legitimate to object to empires. There are, to be sure, still a few examples of empires in the modern world—that is, cases in which certain peoples are being held by larger and culturally distinct powers against their will. China still holds a reluctant Tibet captive, and Russia controls peoples whose cultures and languages have little to do with Russia. The radical scholars who persistently criticize the British Empire are silent about these remaining empires. That is doubtless due to the fact that the Russian and Chinese regimes are closer to the political ideology of the radicals themselves, which the British Empire was not.

Because the Age of Discovery brought together the known and the unknown world, and thus peoples at very different stages of civilizational development, the empires that resulted were fundamentally different from any that had been seen in the past. Up to this point, empires had almost exclusively arisen when one culture took over one or more of its neighbors. The Persians in the 6th century BC simply expanded east, north, and west. The Romans, too, looked to take anything that was adjacent to where they happened to be at a particular time. The Aztec Empire was assembled by expanding outward. Later African empires of the Zulus and the Asante developed in the same way.

The empires that arose during and after the Age of Discovery, however, were quite different. When earlier empires conquered neighboring peoples, there were no great cultural shocks, because the peoples they conquered were, for the most part, at similar stages of development. But when Spaniards sailed thousands of miles away and faced Aztecs, or when the British met African tribes, they were looking at peoples that were not only greatly different to themselves physically, but also at starkly different stages of cultural development.

These new empires would therefore be genuinely diverse collections of people, and it is this fact about the Age of Discovery that makes it so important for the eventual rise of the ideology of *gens una sumus*.

* * * * *

In the early 15th century, the initial stage of the voyages of discovery, the Portuguese explored islands far out in the Atlantic (e.g., the Canaries, the Azores) and went down along the coast of Africa, reaching areas south of the Sahara Desert. This was the first serious contact between Europeans and sub-Saharan Africans. Going further south in 1488, they discovered the sea route around the southern tip of Africa to India and China, and in 1543 they found Japan. It was around the turn of the 15th and 16th centuries that they turned their attention to the Americas.

The Spanish quickly realized what their much smaller neighbor was doing and enlisted the Pope's help to claim the lion's share of what would turn out to be the Americas. The result was the most famous of all Age of Discovery voyages: the discovery of the Americas in 1492 by Christopher Columbus. But Columbus kept to the offshore islands; exploration of the interior of the newly discovered land mass was begun by Hernán Cortés in 1519.

By 1495, northern European nations (the British, French, and Dutch) saw what was going on. Goaded into action by the threat of a stronger Spain, they began their own exploration of the Americas, ignoring the Pope's attempt to split the continent between Spain and Portugal. By 1497 a British expedition was exploring the coast of North America. The Dutch followed the Portuguese route around the southern tip of Africa and discovered Australia in 1606, as well as New Zealand in 1642. By the early 17th century, both the British and the Dutch had settled on the North American coast. By now a great many previously isolated cultures were at last exposed to the rest of the world, but at this stage there was more exploration than settlement. Australia was not settled by Europeans until the late 18th century, and New Zealand not until the early 19th century. Only in America did settlement begin in the early 17th century.

The exploration of Africa went more slowly than anywhere else. North Africa had been well known even in antiquity because it was essentially part of the Mediterranean area, but the territory south of the Sahara Desert was not connected to the contiguous nations that constituted the known world. While the Americas were being explored and settled in the 16th and 17th centuries, European presence in Africa was limited to a series of trading posts along the coast that were established by the Portuguese, British, and Dutch. The Dutch were the first Europeans to settle in and explore the interior of sub-Saharan Africa in the mid-17th century, settling Cape Town in 1652.

The growing Spanish Empire was a collection of disparate far-away lands spread across the globe: in south-east Asia, the Philippine Islands; in Africa, many different territories; and in the Americas large swaths of both North and South America. The Portuguese were in America, Africa, and Asia, and the same was true of the Dutch and the French. The most expansive of all the empires—the British Empire—consisted at its height of territories scattered across every continent and ocean in the world. It was truly said that the sun never set on the British Empire, though much the same could have been said of the Spanish Empire of this early time. These non-contiguous, highly diverse empires were typical of what the Age of Discovery had set in motion.

For the first time, all kinds of cultures at different stages of development mixed with one another, and contact began between peoples who had previously known nothing of one another's existence. How did that affect the way that the different peoples felt about each other? The short-term result was surely a net negative. The tribal attitudes of the known world's peoples, and their disdain for cultures other than their own, would have only become even more pronounced. European sailors and soldiers now saw for the first time the conditions that obtained in the unknown world, a world that had not yet seen the innovations that had spread throughout the known world. Those sailors and soldiers could scarcely have been impressed by what they saw.

The seafarers of the Age of Discovery stood at an apex of technological knowledge and social organization that had been developing for millennia in the known world. The cradle of that world had been the Mediterranean and its surrounding areas. Travel by sea across the Mediterranean was comparatively easy. As a result, new developments and new ideas could spread easily around the Mediterranean, and its different peoples could learn from each other more quickly than anywhere else. That gave the peoples who surrounded the Mediterranean an advantage. The great buildings of the Egyptians were known to the Greeks, who learned from them and developed them further. The first stirrings of a written governmental system in Mesopotamia were probably also known to the Greeks, whose ideas about democracy influenced the Roman Empire and through it the entire Western world. The theological ideas of the Jews influenced first the Romans and then the wider world in the form of Christianity, originally a heretical Jewish sect. Jewish thought even influenced the Muslim world, a people who came to consider Jews their enemy.

As the center of gravity of European civilization began to move north after the Renaissance, northern Europeans began to look to this ancient record of knowledge and thought, developing it further. In the political sphere, the British had begun (in 1215) to develop the crucial idea of limited government with their Magna Carta, and had built upon that in 1265 with Simon de Montfort's parliament—initiating what came to be known as the mother of parliaments. Britons demonstrated the power of that parliament when eventually (in 1648) they deposed and sentenced to death a King (Charles I) who refused to work with it.

All of this meant that Europeans of the Age of Discovery belonged to the most advanced civilization of their time and were heirs to what was already a long tradition of knowledge and social thought, a tradition that had never reached the peoples of the unknown world. It was predictable that the discoverers would have been taken aback by the technological and social primitiveness that they now saw.

The Europeans had been in the iron age for thousands of years, but many of the hitherto isolated cultures with which they now interacted were still in a stone age, with tools of bone and stone. This was true of

Australia, much of Africa, and parts of the Americas. Some American tribes had metallurgy, though it was used mainly for decorative purposes, involving gold, silver, and copper. They didn't have the wheel; neither did the tribes of Australia, or of sub-Saharan Africa. They lacked not only wheeled carts, but also potter's wheels. Only some of these cultures practiced agriculture, and those that did were typically limited to a few crops. Many tribes were still hunter-gatherer societies. Africa was an exception in this regard: farming in sub-Saharan Africa was well established by the Age of Discovery, perhaps because the Sahara, while a barrier to most knowledge from the known world, was not a completely impervious one.

Both from a technological and social point of view, then, these newly discovered cultures could only have seemed a world apart to the people who now found them. Europeans were meeting peoples who were thousands of years behind them: they had no recorded history, virtually no scientific knowledge, and nothing like the administrative complexity and legal stability of European society. They were almost all illiterate (a notable exception is the Mayans of Central America)—not just in the sense that many could neither read nor write, but in the much deeper sense that no writing system for their languages existed at all. These were therefore almost entirely word-of-mouth societies, which severely limited the knowledge that could be passed on from generation to generation. By contrast, though the known world still had plenty of illiterate people, its languages had been written down for hundreds (in some cases thousands) of years.

One particular factor which would have powerfully reinforced the Europeans' feeling of superiority was the ease with which a relatively small number of their explorers and settlers could control much larger native populations. There was a simple explanation for this. By the time of the Age of Discovery, European nations had been fighting each other for a long time, and they had become very good at it. Some of their clashes are legendary: Shakespeare immortalized the Hundred Years' War between England and France in his great play *Henry V* (written *ca.* 1599). The Battle of Agincourt illustrates something important about the development of warfare in Europe. The new technology of the longbow gave the victory to the English against what looked like prohibitive odds. The French had both greater numbers and more heavily armored knights, and yet victory went to the English because of this new weapon.

Similar innovations in weaponry had been a constant feature of European warfare. From the 10th century on, the crossbow was a much-feared weapon. By the early 14th century, the Swiss had discovered that an eighteen-foot pike and a seven-foot halberd could allow an unarmored man to kill with ease any armored man who didn't have those weapons. By the Battle of Agincourt (1415) skilled longbow archers were able to fire rapidly and accurately arrows that could penetrate armor, which meant that they could kill ordinary soldiers wielding only swords and spears before those soldiers got close enough to use their weapons.

But it was the weapons based on gunpowder that really set Europeans above everyone else in warfare. Muskets could strike and kill distant targets, and they did so in ways that would have mystified and terrified native populations that had never seen such weapons. They could take down people who were not even aware that they were at risk, and in a way that must have seemed almost magical. In the 1893 battle of Shangani River, the African Matabele tribe were reported to have thought that the Maxim gun used by the British was the work of an evil spirit.[3] Bullets were therefore as much a psychological weapon as a physical one. To see soldiers dropping for no apparent reason when the enemy was far away must have been both frightening and mystifying. Superiority in weaponry meant that Cortés's small army sometimes went unchallenged; later, as repeating rifles were developed, small British armies were able to control much larger populations in India and China. By the time of the Age of Discovery, Europeans outclassed any non-European state in weaponry by a wide margin.

This technological superiority alone would have increased the customary disdain that explorers—like everyone else of the time—had for peoples other than their own. But it was probably in matters of morality that the seafarers would have been most confident in their own sense of cultural superiority.

Cannibalism was encountered both in the Americas and in Africa. In many places, captives of war were automatically enslaved and then kept either for labor, sexual services, or torture. The latter was a regular form of public entertainment. People who were old or sick were sometimes euthanized. There were public displays of sexual behavior. Europeans also witnessed rituals of human sacrifice. The Christians' reactions to all this can be easily imagined. How could they not have found it distressing?

Modern relativists are wary of saying that one culture is better than another, or that there are advanced and not-so-advanced cultures. They are much offended whenever a people is called "primitive," and they dismiss judgments like these as simply "racist." It's certainly true that many of these tribes had their own kind of complexity. The Tahitians, for example, were master mariners whose ability to undertake long voyages and get where they wanted to go without maps or instruments was quite remarkable.[4] But all of this has nothing to do with the point I am making here, which concerns not how we judge those cultures today, but rather how Europeans of the 16th and 17th centuries must have seen them. The explorers' reaction to the isolated cultures, which up to this time had never been able to learn from the most technologically advanced cultures of the world, was predictable. Europeans must have felt themselves to be on a different footing, both morally and technologically, from the peoples they were encountering. That's not something we can criticize them for, because it was inevitable that they should have thought that way.

In any case, not to distinguish between technologically primitive and technologically advanced cultures at this time would falsify history. It is beyond doubt that the cultures that had been isolated from the waves of innovation that had been sweeping across the contiguous cultures of the known world for millennia would have adopted those innovations, had they been able. Clear proof of this can be seen in what happened after European contact. When these isolated cultures had the chance to do so, they didn't stubbornly stick to their existing conditions, but instead took advantage of the innovations introduced by the European discoverers. They quickly adopted modern technologies, weapons, medicine, travel, and every other aspect of modern life. To judge from their behavior, therefore, they didn't think that their former practices were of equal value to the innovations of modernity.

However, the strongest reason to doubt the position taken by culturally relativist scholars is that they plainly don't believe what they say.

They are just as hostile to the behaviors that appalled the discoverers when they themselves experience those behaviors in the modern world. The plain fact is that, nowadays, nobody is willing to condone torture, cannibalism, ritual murder, or sexual slavery as "alternate life-styles"— least of all the relativists, who are more dogmatic than anyone about, for example, how a society should treat its women.

In the short term, therefore, what the discoverers saw only reinforced their sense of tribal identification. Finding solidarity with the native peoples they now encountered, seeing them as fellow human brothers, was never likely to be their response. Had Europeans already adopted the spirit of *gens una sumus*, they might have understood native customs as conditioned by their physical and social circumstances—but they hadn't, and so they didn't. Instead, they took natives as they found them, by which I mean that they saw the natives' behavior as defining them as peoples. A tribe that behaved in a consistently brutal way was, simply, a brutal people. To European explorers, that was who they were. A tribe that practiced cannibalism would have been judged according to that behavior too. That was the reality that the explorers had to deal with, and that was therefore how they judged the peoples they encountered.

Here we have one of the most important differences between the world of 1500 and that of the present day. Taking people as they were found is very much part and parcel of the outlook of the people of the year 1500. At that time it was a practical necessity to deal with neighboring tribes or countries as they were, not as they might have been. Not to do so would have been dangerous. Of course, that's not how we think now: in the modern world, we are used to the idea that we can separate how peoples seemed to us when first encountered from what they could become or might have been in other circumstances.

What happened in the aftermath of the Second World War illustrates well the transition from the older mode of judgment to the newer one. Survivors of that war's Battle of Midway, both Japanese and American, now meet and enjoy each other's company as fellow warriors and survivors, though during the war soldiers of the Allies who were prisoners of the Japanese army commonly saw the Japanese as a cruel and sadistic race. They now take a different view. They understand that how the Japanese acted in the Second World War is not what defines them as human beings. They were at that time part of a warrior culture that reached back to the Middle Ages, and their behavior was determined by that culture. In the meantime, their culture has changed.

In the 18th century, no drastic transition from a tribalist to a post-tribal ideology had yet taken place, and so there was no choice but to understand unfamiliar peoples as they were when first encountered. That led early European settlers in America, for example, to make what now seem rather harsh judgments of the native tribes they encountered. Thomas Jefferson famously spoke of American Indians in the Declaration of Independence as "the merciless Indian savages, whose known rule of warfare, is an undistinguished destruction of all ages, sexes and conditions." That statement might now seem disconcerting, but it's not so once we understand that it reflected the near-universal habit of the time of taking people as they were when first encountered. When putting their names to this opinion, neither Jefferson nor any of the other signers gave much thought to the possibility that this behavior was not the whole story of who these people were, or that in other circumstances they might have behaved quite differently. In the modern world, we don't immediately assume that the people Jefferson was talking about are innately immoral. We look beyond their present conditions, seeing them as products of circumstance, because we are sure that those people share with us a common humanity.

As the Japanese survivors of the Battle of Midway demonstrate, today we have an advantage that those earlier peoples didn't: we have seen how the lineal descendants of formerly fearsome people developed. As modernity overtook them, they adapted to its values. And so it is with the descendants of Jefferson's "merciless Indian savages": they, too, no longer slaughter whole families of their enemies. We've changed our view of them accordingly, but that does not mean that we have a right to condemn historical figures for taking particular peoples as they found them. Many modern scholars see Jefferson's remark about "merciless Indian savages" as proof of his racism, but it isn't. His was a practical judgment, typical not just of Americans, but of almost everyone at that time, before the spirit of *gens una sumus* had taken hold.

As contact between the known and unknown worlds gradually reduced the discrepancies between the societal development of different cultures, we'd eventually discover that, indeed, we are all much more alike than we used to think. But the people of many centuries ago could never have afforded to think this way. For their own safety, they had to act in light of what they saw. When a particular tribe treated them savagely, they had to respond accordingly. And when Europeans encountered people who had been isolated from the known world's thousands of years of development, they described those people as "primitive," because that was how they appeared to Europeans. Given that the philosophy of *gens una sumus* played almost no role in 1500 and long after, a charge of racism against Europeans of that time would make no sense, because it would have to be leveled equally at everyone, of whatever tribe.

How did this habit of taking people as they were initially found gradually weaken? As the Age of Discovery developed into the high colonial period, it was Christian missionaries who took the longer view. They assumed that, regardless of how a people may have appeared at first contact, there was a commonality between these newly discovered peoples and themselves. They not only believed, but acted on their belief, that those people were not defined by what they first saw of them. They assumed that all human beings were capable of the same civilized behavior, once educated to that end. These missionaries are now much criticized for their allegedly blinkered insistence on their own value systems, yet the fact remains that the belief that was basic to all that they did—the ideology of *gens una sumus*—is the same belief that animates their modern critics. And they were among the first to live whole-heartedly by that idea.

Yet this perspective of the missionaries was not prevalent at the beginning of the Age of Discovery or for some time afterwards. The first European explorers took peoples as they encountered them, just as Jefferson and his colleagues did: when they came upon cannibals, they saw them as savages. Because much of what they saw horrified them, they were unable to experience a sense of oneness with native peoples as fellow human beings.

For their part, the European explorers didn't remember how long it had taken for their own traditions and ethical standards to develop, and how much effort had gone into forging them. The societies they belonged to had slowly managed to tame at least some of man's worst impulses, but that process belonged to a distant past that was beyond their recall.

One specific case of Europeans taking indigenous populations as they were found needs special mention, because its effects are still with us. As we've seen, early European contact with Africans occurred neither by exploration of the interior of Africa, nor by settlement. This contact began only with a series of trading posts on the west coast of Africa. Even the seafaring explorers knew virtually nothing of functioning African societies, because their first experience of Africans were those who had been enslaved by Muslim traders, and who were destined to be involuntary agricultural laborers.

If the European explorers were already inclined to see themselves as belonging to a culture superior to any they had encountered—and at this period of history, that could hardly have been otherwise—their initial impressions of Africans could only have been that these were, of all the peoples they had encountered, the most physically and socially distinct from themselves. Today, we can understand how artificial the impression created by that first encounter was, but the voyagers of the Age of Discovery could not. At a time in which unsympathetic tribalism still prevailed everywhere, and with no previous experience whatsoever of sub-Saharan African people, the Europeans exhibited an entirely predictable reaction. We should not be surprised that, on the basis of this first encounter, Europeans saw Africans as a race apart, even an inferior race.

Only radical activists with an axe to grind could think that this demonstrates racism on the part of those Europeans of the time. To be sure, this initial attitude towards Africans would have a long history. Yet what should engage our attention here is not the understandable reaction of Europeans to this first encounter, but how soon and how radically their attitudes began to change. For, as we'll see, the groundswell of a movement to transcend tribalism in general, and tribalism towards Africans in particular, originated among these very same Europeans, and nowhere else.

A crucial fact about the first permanent settlement of English-speaking peoples in North America was that it took place shortly after the beginning of the 17th century, over a hundred years before European settlements in other areas of the world began. That time difference is of enormous importance. In 1500, the ideology of *gens una sumus* didn't yet exist, and there had been no significant adoption of the ideology by 1619. It was in that context that Europeans both met Africans for the first time and settled in North America. By the time the next major round of European colonial settlements began—in the late-18th and early-19th centuries—a major change in attitudes to other peoples was already well underway. As we'll see in the next chapter, the move beyond the tribalism of 1500 to the philosophy of *gens una sumus* began in Great Britain.

We can only judge adequately what happened in the years between 1500 and the present day if we constantly keep an eye on the extent to which *gens una sumus* had succeeded in making inroads into the long-standing rule of tribalism. When a North American tribe massacred entire settlements of Europeans, this left a lasting impression. Similarly, the circumstances in which Europeans first met Africans left an impression that was difficult to dispel. In both cases, the triumph of the spirit of *gens una sumus* eventually dissolved those initial impressions. Anyone who now watches Fox News routinely sees a whole series of brilliant Black commentators analyzing the news of the day: Harris Faulkner, Leo Terrell, Candace Owens, Rob Smith, Star Parker, Lawrence Jones, Charles Payne, David Webb, Tyrus, Allen West, Larry Elder, Bob Woodson, Byron Donalds, Deroy Murdock, Ben Carson, Ted Williams, and many others.

And yet the list of prominent Westerners who were still under the influence of those first impressions reached far into the future, including people who, in their own day, counted as enlightened, responsible, and compassionate. They include Thomas Jefferson, Voltaire, David Hume, Charles Darwin, Woodrow Wilson, and Theodore Roosevelt, among many others. No, they were certainly not "racists," as we understand that term now. To call them so would be anachronistic. They were simply among the great majority who were still under the lasting cultural influence of those first impressions.

It did not help that many societies within Africa generally remained isolated from the known world longer than almost any other people. Africa was known as "The Dark Continent" because both the landscape and the peoples of its interior were not well understood until well into the 19th century. To this day, literacy rates in sub-Saharan Africa are still the lowest in the world: 68 percent for men; 52 percent for women. As we'll see, colonialism helped to bring the formerly isolated cultures of Africa into the wider system of the known world, allowing them to begin to absorb the innovations that had built up there over thousands of years. But the high colonial period in Africa was very short, lasting less than a century. Elsewhere, colonialism had more time to do its work, and the discrepancy still shows.

It would be the thinkers of the British Enlightenment who began the public debate about the nature of humanity that moved us decisively in the direction of *gens una sumus*. In so doing, they naturally broached the question that had not occurred to the early explorers of the Age of Discovery: did the cultural conditions of an isolated population really define them as human beings? The growth of literacy, and the British Enlightenment that resulted from it, constitutes the second major event in the transition from 1500 to the present day. How it unfolded is the subject of the following chapter.

Chapter Three: The Crucial Spread of Literacy, and of Ideas

W E'VE SEEN THAT in the world of 1500 AD, different peoples knew so little of one another that, far from having sympathy for other peoples, they were more inclined to fear them. Further, we've seen that the early stages of the Age of Discovery did nothing to improve that state of affairs, and, if anything, made it somewhat worse. Yet as the 17th century progressed, something began to develop that would eventually change this picture considerably: the first steps toward widespread literacy. This would mean the creation of a reading public, which in turn would make public opinion a far more powerful factor in human life. With widening literacy, ideas could reach ever more people—though not nearly as many as would eventually be the case when television, radio, and the internet could disseminate them more rapidly and widely than ever.

Throughout recorded history, individual thinkers have occasionally broached the issue of our common humanity, but before the printing press their ideas could have reached only a very small number of people. The closest thing to a wide dissemination of thought would have been through use of the pulpits of the Christian churches, where some priests would certainly have spoken of all people as equally God's children. But to judge from the results, this didn't dissuade people from their inherited tribalism to any great extent. They still identified with their own, and they were still uniquely concerned with the good of their people. Even when a sermon spoke of a common humanity, this was largely understood as referring to the listener's community. This restricted sense of a commonality with other human beings was not only felt by ordinary people. Most priests saw things in much the same way. In wars between states and cultures, the clergy could be as partisan as anyone else.

After Gutenberg's invention of the printing press, books, pamphlets, and eventually newspapers began to appear in growing numbers, and to be read by a widening public. More people than ever before were gaining access to information and opinion of all kinds, both practical and theoretical. People who were able to read could form their own ideas about what they had read, and they could exchange their opinions with other readers. All of this is important for our story for many reasons. Printed matter could spread knowledge of the wider world and of other peoples, and that would begin to reduce the ignorance that had inclined everyone to suspicion of other peoples. It could also spread technological and scientific knowledge, which in the long run would reduce the disparity between the levels of development and living standards of different societies. But those were the longer-term effects of literacy. An altogether different consequence would move somewhat more quickly: the rise of the ideology of *gens una sumus*.

The most immediate and important result of the spread of literacy was that it facilitated discussion and dissemination of what we might loosely call ideas about morality—that is, ideas about how human life should be conducted: about right and wrong, about society, about character, about responsibility, about the proper form of government. All of this began to create the possibility of a vibrant public opinion, and consequently of a public conscience. Literacy meant that the impact of public opinion would no longer be restricted to local settings; it could now become a force with a much greater reach. Literacy sets the stage for manifestos, petitions, even widespread campaigns for or against things that shocked the public's conscience. Literacy provides a country with the means of debating its values.

Without literacy and printed materials, public opinion could never have achieved this heightened degree of force, but with them it now becomes something distinctly to be reckoned with. Before long, a particularly serious issue would become one of the first *causes célèbres* that engaged this newly empowered public: the campaign to abolish slavery. But that was just one aspect of a growing move in the direction of *gens una sumus*.

How did this new means of discussing moral questions develop, and when? There are two distinct parts to that question. The first is: how and where did publishing develop? And the second is: how and where did literacy develop? In 1500 there was little of both. As they developed, the one naturally depended upon the other.

Woodcut printing had been known in antiquity, so the idea of duplicating written material was not itself new. Even movable type was already developed by around 1000 AD. But what Johannes Gutenberg invented in 1455 was the beginning of modern book production: a movable type printing press with metal characters. Books created in this way soon afforded much broader access to the knowledge we have inherited from our past. The entire legacy of classical (Greek and Roman) antiquity became available in book form within the first half century of Gutenberg's invention. The wisdom of the ancient world was thus now disseminated as never before, but this dissemination was still limited to those who could afford books, and to those who could read them. Gutenberg certainly made books cheaper than they had been, but they were still at first prohibitively expensive for ordinary people: the cost of one book could feed a family for some time. Thus, the countries that were most prosperous were also the ones in which the production of books, magazines, and newspapers would advance most rapidly. And at this time in history, that points us to northern Europe.

The European Renaissance—the rediscovery of the legacy of ancient Greece and Rome—began in southern Europe, particularly in Italy, but by 1600 it was clear that the center of European learning was shifting to the north, as prosperity was increasing faster there than elsewhere. The corruption of the Catholic Church had led to the spread of Protestantism, and with this northern Europe became independent of Catholic orthodoxy in thought and science. Popes had often tried to squelch liberalizing political developments in England that they didn't like (Magna Carta is a case in point), but their power there was lost after King Henry VIII severed the English Church from Rome. There was much more to the Protestant split than northern Europe's simply going its own way in theological doctrine. The Protestants did something that immediately helped to set northern Europe on a path to dominance over the south: they began to translate the Bible into their own national languages and to make those translations available to laymen. As early as 1539, Henry VIII decreed that a Bible in the English language must be placed in every Christian church and made available for parishioners to read. That gave every Christian an incentive to learn to read, and every Protestant government a reason to encourage literacy. A literate citizenry was always going to be a more productive and prosperous one. Because the Protestant countries were the first to attain widespread literacy, their already-increasing prosperity was further enhanced.

It was in Britain that a sizable reading public first arose. Britain's political traditions had gradually allotted the ordinary person more individual freedom since Magna Carta (1215) and the first Parliament (1265). The Civil War of 1642–51 and the "Glorious Revolution" of 1688 established forever the relative liberty of the British subject. By modern standards there was still a long way to go, but by the standards of the time British citizens were now freer than those of any other country. This political liberty opened a space for individuals to use their minds and bodies to better their conditions. That made for more innovation and even greater prosperity. The gradual adoption of democratic and limited government released the energies and imaginations of British citizens to a degree unmatched elsewhere.

The fact that books and pamphlets were already impacting British society by the middle of the 17th century can be inferred from the publication in 1644 of the most celebrated of all treatises on the freedom of the press, John Milton's *Areopagitica*. Surprisingly, this was still some twenty years before the first British newspaper began publication, but pamphleteering had already been well established. The Cornell University philosopher George Sabine sums up the importance of Milton's treatise: "Its basic principle was the right and also the duty of every intelligent man as a rational being, to know the grounds and take responsibility for his beliefs and actions. Its corollary was a society and a state in which decisions are reached by open discussion, in which the sources of information are not contaminated by authority in the interest of party, and in which political unity is secured not by force but by a consensus that respects variety of opinion."[1] It would be hard to imagine such a statement concerning, say, the France of this time, with its absolute monarchy.

Milton envisaged a society in which, by means of a free press, and only by that means, a literate and informed public could freely discuss the issues of the day, great and small. It was precisely this literate British public that was to play such an important part in the development of ideas about the conduct of life, ideas that would include both the specific case of opposition to slavery and the broader question of how peoples behaved toward each other.

But how widespread was literacy in Britain in these times? Estimates vary. In his outstanding book *Inventing Freedom*, Daniel Hannan gives a fairly high estimate: "In 1600, 35 percent of Englishmen were able to read. By 1700, the figure was 60 percent (25 percent for Englishwomen.)"[2] Other modern scholars put the figure somewhat lower than this, but it seems safe to say that more than half of the English people were literate by some point between the late-17th and early-18th century. This means that while few people were literate in 1500, within two centuries a very large reading public had developed.

A different but equally compelling way to grasp the magnitude of the change is to look at the development of newspapers and magazines in 17th-century Britain. The first English newspaper was the *London Gazette*, which began publication in 1665 under the name of the *Oxford Gazette*. Only sixty years later, by the 1720s, there were twelve London newspapers and twenty-four provincial papers, in addition to about ten periodicals. We can add to this the fact that access to books became suddenly much cheaper with the introduction of lending libraries in 1740. The speed at which British newspapers and magazines were established in the late 17th century is not matched anywhere else.

The vigorous early growth of the English novel yet again tells the story of the rapid rise of a strong reading public. The 17th and 18th centuries already witnessed the creation of many great works in the history of English literature. To name only the most prominent among them: John Bunyan's *The Pilgrim's Progress* (1688); Daniel Defoe's *Robinson Crusoe* (1719) and *Moll Flanders* (1722); Jonathan Swift's *Gulliver's Travels* (1726); Samuel Richardson's *Pamela* (1740) and *Clarissa* (1748); Henry Fielding's *Joseph Andrews* (1742) and *Tom Jones* (1749). If we look at the progress of the novel in France or Germany at this early time, there is nothing like this profusion of great names.

Novels, too, are one of the ways in which a society discusses the value and purpose of human life, as well as right and wrong behavior. These early novels are much concerned with sin and virtue, with responsible and irresponsible behavior, and so they, too, became an important arena for the national conversation about morality. Bunyan's *The Pilgrim's Progress* is explicitly an allegorical moral fable, while Swift's *Gulliver's Travels* is a satirical commentary on almost all aspects of human life, but especially politics. Richardson's *Pamela* and *Clarissa* are about the perils ordinary young women face on their treacherous journey toward the safe-haven of marriage. Fielding's *Tom Jones* is a tug of war between a full-throated enjoyment of life on the one hand, and the rules that keep it on an even keel on the other. By contrast, the great French novel of this time—Madame de Lafayette's *La Princesse de Clèves*—is not about the lives of ordinary people, but instead those of French aristocrats. Its central issue is a fastidious extreme of virtue rarely encountered in reality. The only lasting German novel of the period—Hans Jakob Christoffel von Grimmelshausen's *Simplicius Simplicissimus*—is a picaresque tale of the chaos and suffering of the Thirty Years' War. Its focus is not so much on morality as on survival.

It is Daniel Defoe's *Robinson Crusoe*, however, that is most relevant for our story, because its central feature is the cooperation and even friendship between a European and a Black man. Radical modern scholars look at this and deplore the subordinate position the Black man takes to the White—for them this is an original instance of White supremacy and oppression. But this way of looking at the novel violates the crucial principle set out at the beginning of my first chapter: those radicals are measuring Defoe against the conditions of the 21st century, not those in place before and while his book was written. Thus they miss what is remarkable here, which is a relationship that begins to take us beyond the instinctive tribalism of 1500. In *Robinson Crusoe*, a White man and a Black man depend on each other, cooperate with each other, and defend each other. With Defoe we are on the road to the future.

Women were initially literate at a rate that was about half that of men, but they soon began to catch up, and they became more voracious readers of novels than men. Middle-class women had far more time to read novels because they were still barred from many male pursuits, both in business and leisure.

By the mid-18th century, the British reading public was more extensive than that of any other major European nation. France was probably the closest, but it lacked the kind of middle-class moral debate witnessed in Britain for several reasons. First, France was a Catholic country, and the Catholic Church was still hostile to public access to translations of the Bible into the vernacular. The first French translations had to be printed outside France, and it was not until the Revolutionary Era that the Bible in French became available within the country's borders. The clergy didn't trust ordinary people to discuss by themselves the moral issues raised in the Bible.

The second factor which limited discussion in France was its absolute monarchy, which suppressed the discussion of social and moral issues according to its own whim. No *Areopagitica* there. This restriction slowed the development of the kind of reading public that had emerged in Britain. The third and perhaps most important factor was that most of the French intelligentsia of this time shared the disdain that both the Church and the monarchy had for the lower classes. The moral issues that obsessed the "*philosophes*" were anti-clericalism and anti-monarchism. The most famous of those *philosophes*, Voltaire (1694–1778), was a minor aristocrat whose overriding dream was to abolish both the Church and the monarchy, but who didn't seem to care much about improving the lot of the common man. In fact, Voltaire despised the common people and referred to them as a "canaille"—a rabble. Far from experiencing a fellow-feeling for people of other cultures, Voltaire couldn't even find that kind of feeling for his own countrymen.

The second most famous French *philosophe* of the time, Jean-Jacques Rousseau (1712–1778), had a communist view of private property. For him, property was the source of all evil. But the abolition of private property would scarcely have improved the material conditions of ordinary French people, and it would certainly have impeded the development of a prosperous middle class akin to that which was rising in Britain.

As Gertrude Himmelfarb observes in her groundbreaking book, *The Roads to Modernity: The British, French, and American Enlightenments*, "The British did not have *philosophes*. They had moral philosophers, a very different breed."[3] Rousseau's influence didn't make the French freer, but instead only led them to lurch from one tyranny to another. Meanwhile, the British were developing an economic system of free trade that was incompatible with Rousseau's radical egalitarianism. The prosperity which emerged from that free trade helped to promote the literacy necessary for a vibrant discussion of moral issues, and for the development of a public opinion.

The German contribution to the European Enlightenment was limited by its lateness. The appalling destruction caused by the Thirty Years' War meant that the German Renaissance would be delayed to the last half of the 18th century, long after Milton and Locke started the discussion that soon became so lively and extensive in Britain.

In any case, English philosophy was generally more practical, more rooted in the reality of human life, than the philosophies of continental Europe. The conventional labels attached to the different philosophies of both areas have long been "continental rationalism" and "English empiricism." These have always seemed to me inadequate terms. All of us aspire to being rational rather than irrational, and these conventional labels seem therefore to give the continentals the edge. Yet the greatest British philosophers of the period—John Locke (1632–1704) and David Hume (1711–1776)—are highly rational, down-to-earth, and for that reason influential writers. The term "rationalism" as applied to continental philosophers like Gottfried Wilhelm Leibniz (1646–1716), Baruch Spinoza (1632–1677), and Immanuel Kant (1724–1804) implies something much more specific, and limited, than that word (which sounds like a first cousin of "reasonable") usually seems to mean. In this context, "rationalism" refers not to reasonableness, but to closed logical systems that attempt to deduce everything *a priori*, that is, from supposed first principles—propositions that allegedly can't be doubted —rather than from the observed (i.e., empirical) facts of life. In the long run, all those systems became failures that no longer exert serious influence on philosophical discussions in the modern era, largely because those first principles couldn't do the work that was demanded of them. By contrast, Locke and Hume are still very much a living part of the modern philosophical conversation.

In Britain, John Locke set the discussion off in a way that was very different from Voltaire, consumed as the latter was by his antipathy toward almost everything in ordinary French life. Locke began directly with reflections on the essential nature and rights of "man," rather than specific groups of men. The beginning of the second chapter of his *Second Treatise of Government* (1690) illustrates well the way Locke constructs a train of thought:

> To understand political power right, and derive it from its
> original, we must consider, what state all men are naturally in,
> and that is, a state of perfect freedom to order their actions,
> and dispose of their possessions and persons, as they think fit,
> within the bounds of the law of nature, without asking leave, or
> depending upon the will of any other man. A state also of equal-
> ity, wherein all the power and jurisdiction is reciprocal, no one
> having more than another; there being nothing more evident,
> than that creatures of the same species and rank, promiscuously
> born to all the same advantages of nature, and the use of the
> same faculties, should also be equal one amongst another
> without subordination or subjection, unless the lord and master
> of them all should, by any manifest declaration of his will, set
> one above another, and confer on him, by an evident and clear
> appointment, an undoubted right to dominion and sovereignty.

Locke soon gets to a principle that, if taken seriously by his readers, must turn their minds to the matter of slavery:

> The state of nature has a law of nature to govern it, which oblig-
> es every one: and reason, which is that law, teaches all mankind,
> who will but consult it, that being all equal and independent, no
> one ought to harm another in his life, health, liberty, or posses-
> sions: for men being all the workmanship of one omnipotent,
> and infinitely wise maker; all the servants of one sovereign
> master, sent into the world by his order, and about his business;
> they are his property, whose workmanship they are, made to
> last during his, not one another's pleasure: and being furnished
> with like faculties, sharing all in one community of nature, there
> cannot be supposed any such subordination among us, that may

authorize us to destroy one another, as if we were made for one another's uses, as the inferior ranks of creatures are for our's.

Here is already the idea that every individual human being has his or her own place in creation, and is equally free and independent, all being equally the work of their creator, so that they may not be used simply for the purposes of another. We should note, again, that this is not the kind of abstract general statement about the rights of man found among the French *philosophes*. Those thinkers were talking about peoples being freed from the grip of tyrannical rulers, which is the thrust of Rousseau's famous beginning to his treatise Du Contrat Social: "L'homme est né libre, et partout il est dans les fers." ("Man is born free, and everywhere he is in chains.") Locke's point is very different. He is talking about one individual harmed by another—that is, one person being reduced to whatever another obliges him to be. Again, Gertrude Himmelfarb gets to Locke's fundamental point: "The moral sense and common sense that the British attributed to all individuals gave to all people, including the common people, a common humanity and a common fund of moral and social obligations."[4] To put the matter another way, Locke is essentially explaining the implications of the philosophy of gens una sumus.

Inevitably, widening literacy meant that these discussions were also informed by older traditions, traditions such as Athenian democracy, or the moral world of the Jewish Bible. But the specific shape that these ideas took in Locke's text spoke to the stage of development that the world had now reached. This is why those ideas would eventually become so influential beyond Britain.

Locke was soon followed by a host of other British writers who developed further this concern with moral ideas, particularly ideas about our duty to our fellow man. The most influential of them was Anthony Ashley Cooper, 3rd Earl of Shaftesbury (1671–1713), who was widely read both in his native Britain and on the continent of Europe. Central to Shaftesbury's thought was the idea that we all have a moral sense, a "sense of right and wrong," and that this sense is turned toward the common good, the good not of the self but of the whole of mankind. One of the many who joined in this national discussion was Francis

Hutcheson (1694–1746). Hutcheson extended this idea of the common good with the phrase "the greatest happiness for the greatest numbers." This was the spirit that informed British moral philosophers throughout the rest of the 18th century and beyond.

What was happening here did not stop with mere theorizing. Philanthropy became a serious factor in British national life, and many charities were soon founded, most of them aimed at improving the lot of the poor. The moral discussions surrounding that development soon led to the classic distinction between the deserving poor (people who work hard but are down on their luck) and the undeserving poor (lazy good-for-nothings) in the Poor Law of 1834, an early statement of the great dilemma of social reformers, which remains relevant to this day.

Today it's often said that the Enlightenment thinkers talked a great deal about the rights of man, but that when they did so they were really thinking about White people like themselves, not Africans or Asians. History shows conclusively that this was not so. One of the most celebrated of the British Enlightenment thinkers, Edmund Burke, persuaded the House of Commons to impeach Warren Hastings (Governor-General of India from 1773 to 1785) because, among other crimes, he had trampled on the rights of the Indian people. Burke gave several specific examples, the most compelling of which was Hastings's having colluded in the cruel "extirpation" of the Rohilla people. A lengthy process that lasted several years was proof that the matter was taken seriously by the Commons. Here an Enlightenment thinker was speaking passionately and to great effect about the rights of a race other than his own or that of his audience, and he was being taken very seriously by that audience. The issue agitated no less a body than the mother of parliaments for several years.

But the most compelling proof that as the 18th century progressed the British were beginning to think about the rights of all human beings, not just White Europeans, was that it was precisely in Britain, *and in no other place at this time*, that the movement to abolish slavery developed, and developed very quickly. Locke was already widely read, and consequently the broad dissemination of his idea that the life of every individual has its own rationale, and that one person may not be used for the purposes of another, had begun to create a fertile ground within the British reading public for a movement to abolish slavery.

To the modern reader, these ideas may by now seem so familiar as to be no more than commonplace. But that is so only because their adoption in the modern world has been so complete that they no longer seem novel. In Locke's time, however, they were far from commonplace, and we can only understand the history of our civilization if we grasp that it was at this point that they began to exert real and widespread influence for the first time. This was where the ideology of *gens una sumus* began to gather steam. And we must never forget that it was the prosperity produced by Britain's relatively free markets, together with the literacy that this prosperity made possible, that allowed that ideology to arise and flourish.

To understand how unique the abolitionist movement was, and how important it was historically, we need to look briefly at its historical background. Slavery had always been a worldwide phenomenon. Until the Middle Ages, no group of people can be considered morally superior to any other in this respect. In different societies across the world, captives of war were often enslaved. There was no organized movement against slavery anywhere until the Christian Church (therefore mainly Europeans) began to oppose it, and the practice of slavery began to end in Europe as the attitude of the Church spread. An initial result was the development of a general feeling that members of the same religion should not enslave one another, but this meant that Christians, Muslims, and Jews alike all justified enslaving members of other religions. One result of the Crusades, for example, was the enslavement of thousands of Muslims and of Christians. Pagans were, of course, fair game for everyone, because they were nobody's co-religionists.

In England, the Church Council of London in 1102 called traffic in slaves "an infamous business," and forbade it. By 1200, slavery was virtually at an end in England. There was never any legislation to ban it, but a series of later court cases (for example, in 1569 and 1701) repeatedly confirmed that it was inconsistent with common law and the principle of *habeas corpus*. The Irish Church was also strongly opposed to slavery by the end of the 12th century, and the Popes began to oppose it in the later Middle Ages. By the 13th century Scandinavia had abolished slavery, as had France by 1300. European nations were, however, alone in having thus ended slavery by the late Middle Ages.

As the British developed their movement to abolish slavery worldwide in the 18th century, the general shape both of practice and opinion in the world was that a few nations, all European, had turned against it, while the great majority of peoples hadn't, most of whom continued to practice it without hesitation. It's worth noting that this general picture is starkly at variance with the one that modern radicals want to paint. The peoples they vehemently condemn are the very ones who were promoting reform, and the peoples they lionize are those who continued to practice slavery until the European-led abolition movement finally caught up with them too—that is, Africans, Asians, the native peoples of the Americas, and others.

When the Spanish and Portuguese began transporting the first African slaves to the Americas in 1526, it marked a break with what had been the status quo, at least in many parts of Europe. While Europe itself remained largely free of slaves, the trans-Atlantic slave trade, initiated by southern European nations, began. By 1600, several hundred thousand African slaves had been transported across the Atlantic by the Spanish and Portuguese.

In the English-speaking colonies of North America, however, there seems to have been no deliberate and planned commencement of the slave trade. A Portuguese slave ship was captured by an English privateer in 1619, and the twenty slaves on board were taken. Once this original group of slaves was sold to English settlers in the Virginia colony, efforts were taken to get more. These settlers knew that slavery was not allowed in their native land, but once having started the practice, they kept going.

Slavery had therefore been practiced for a hundred years in the Americas before the English colonists took to it. Colonial Brazil imported more slaves than any other society in the Americas, and present-day Haiti, Cuba, Jamaica, Mexico, and Puerto Rico all saw slavery introduced during the 16th century. Slavery had, accordingly, long been a way of life in all the lands surrounding the British colonies before the capture of that Portuguese ship set the English settlers on a path contrary to the practice of their native country for the last four hundred years.

Both the physical distance from England and the prevalence of slavery throughout the Americas must have been partly responsible for the English settlers' letting a particular opportunity lead them into something that was no longer permitted in England. Another circumstance that might have contributed to their ignoring the prevailing English attitude was that the African slaves they saw in all the lands around them had already been enslaved by other Africans.

Regardless of all these contributing factors, however, there is one fundamental and overriding question that must be asked and answered before we can judge these English settlers for taking in slaves: at this point in history, whose value system were they contravening? The answer to this is clear: they contravened the values of their native England, and of some of its close neighbors, but of no other peoples. They were certainly not violating the law and practice of Africa, where slavery still flourished without opposition and would continue do so for many centuries to come. Nor were they offending the values of Asia or of the Americas. They were in fact not transgressing against the values of any society on earth at the time *except* those of their own European culture. Given the state of the world at this time, if we are to criticize the English settlers, we should have to invoke the values that prevailed only in that unique culture, and the values of its Christian Church. And we should remember that even in Great Britain, the campaign to abolish slavery worldwide had not yet begun in 1619.

Yet above all, in considering the actions of these British settlers what is most important is that we keep an eye on the difference between the world of 1619 and the world of today. The world of 1619 was one in which the safety and survival of one's own people was the most pressing of anyone's concerns in a dangerous world. The spirit of *gens una sumus* was not yet present anywhere, and consequently, what we would now call racism was nothing but the tribal practicality that was ubiquitous in these early times.

Moreover, none of this should divert us from the crucial fact that, later in that same century, moral philosophers in Britain, and Britain alone, began to create a climate of opinion that developed into a strong consensus against slavery. Public opinion was clearly the driving force. No less a philosopher than David Hume wrote that the opinions of ordinary people are more to be trusted in matters of morality than philosophers: "For it must be observed, that the opinions of men, in this case, carry with them a peculiar authority, and are, in a great measure, infallible."[5] By the last half of the 18th century the pressure of British public opinion against slavery was overwhelming.

Though slaves were on occasion brought to England by their masters, no trading in them being allowed, a court case in 1772 made it also illegal to hold a slave there. The result was that from this time onward, anyone who brought a slave to England was effectively freeing him. In 1777, John Wesley, the highly influential founder of Methodism, wrote his *Thoughts Upon Slavery*, a strongly argued case for abolition. Wesley was adamant: "I absolutely deny all slaveholding to be consistent with any degree of even natural justice." And he addressed slaveholders in withering terms: "Are you *a man?* Then you should have an *human* heart. But have you indeed? What is your heart made of? Is there no such principle as compassion there? Do you never *feel* another's pain? Have you no sympathy? No sense of human woe? No pity for the miserable?"[6] The two greatest writers of the Scottish Enlightenment, David Hume and Adam Smith, both added to the growing anti-slavery sentiment.

This increasing power of public opinion created by the steadily expanding reading public exerted considerable influence, even across the thousands of miles separating England from its American colonies. In 1777, Vermont declared slavery illegal. Pennsylvania followed suit in 1780. In 1783 the first organized movement to end slavery more broadly began when English Quakers presented a petition to Parliament. The culmination of these efforts was the founding, by William Wilberforce in 1787, of the Society for Effecting Abolition of the Slave Trade. By 1804 all the northern states had abolished slavery. In 1807 Britain abolished slavery throughout its empire. Not only that: as Daniel Hannan observes, "The United Kingdom persuaded or bullied other European states, as well as African rulers, into agreeing to halt the transatlantic trade, and the Royal Navy was deployed against the slavers."[7] The British Navy became the international anti-slavery police force.

There was nothing remotely comparable anywhere else: not in Europe, not in Asia, not in Africa, not in the Americas. The critical sequence of events is clear: the relative political freedom of the British created an affluent middle class; that middle class, in turn, generated a large reading public; that reading public began to concern itself with moral issues; that concern led to a powerful public sentiment that was hostile to slavery, to the point of militancy.

This growth of anti-slavery sentiment, however, was just one particular result of the British reading public's interest in morality. More generally, widespread discussions of human rights and a host of other moral questions were slowly creating a new climate of opinion concerning one culture's relation to another. Perhaps this reflected Britain's growing confidence as its empire grew increasingly formidable. The suspicion and hostility that had been the default condition of the year 1500 were gradually being replaced by a more benign attitude—a growing sense that the various peoples within the British Empire had their own claims and their own rationale. The spirit of *gens una sumus* was making serious progress.

The eventual global importance of what began in Britain can't be overstated, but we can fully grasp its magnitude only if we remember the principle that I set out in my first chapter: these developments must be measured against the world of 1500, not that of the present day. Modern scholars tend to look back on the activities of the British abolitionists of the late 18th century and the related actions of the northerly American states with a distinctly holier-than-thou attitude: at long last, the narrative goes, they came to their senses and adopted the right values! That way of putting the matter assumes that those values were or should have been always present. But that's an assumption which renders unintelligible the groundbreaking significance of abolitionist thought and activism.

If instead we look at these same events against the world of 1500, we can't fail to see how fundamentally revolutionary they were. British 18th-century opinion, initiated by a small number of key thinkers but achieving decisive force because of an increasingly literate society, was leading the entire world beyond the prevailing attitudes of 1500. Under their influence, our modern ethos of *gens una sumus* was taking center stage for the first time. British public opinion of this era is the *fons et origo* of modern values as regards the relations between different peoples, and certainly with respect to the matter of slavery. It's even the ultimate source of the ridiculous modern caricature of those values which we now call wokeness. Yes, even that foolish and degenerate parody of modern moral values derives from this earlier British debate, since it's essentially parasitic upon the British thinkers of the 17th and 18th centuries.

This, then, is where our modern attitudes first emerge and gain strength amid a background of continuing tribalism in the rest of the world. It was the greatest achievement of the British Enlightenment. The British didn't at long last stumble into correct values, as their modern detractors want us to believe: *they created them!* And, having done so, they eventually gave them to the rest of the world, though not without considerable resistance from peoples beyond the Anglosphere.

The British weren't content just to pronounce slavery illegal: they went to war against it, and effectively ended the slave trade on the western coast of Africa. British naval vessels stopped and searched any ships departing from West Africa that were suspected of carrying slaves. That the world's greatest navy was deployed in this way was astonishing, and it demonstrated a commitment and a degree of seriousness about opposition to slavery that no other country has ever come close to matching, at least until their cousins in the northern United States fought a war against it in 1861. Even in the face of this British naval war against slavery, Africans were still determined to continue it. When the Royal Navy shut the slave trade down on the African west coast, African slavers turned instead to their east coast, making it the new center of the slave trade. Thus, millions more enslaved Africans were sent east by Africans themselves, for many years thereafter.[8]

The value system that led to the abolition of slavery was therefore unambiguously that of the British—certainly not that of the Africans, who stubbornly persisted in their slave-trading despite British efforts to curtail it. If 18th-century British people hadn't discussed these matters so fervently and come to a public consensus about them, nobody would have. In that case, the abolitionist movement would have taken much longer to coalesce, and the road to our modern ethos of *gens una sumus* would have also been far less direct.

Chapter Four: The Changing Rationale for Empire

WHAT HAD HAPPENED during the 18th century in Britain was the first major assertion of what would eventually become a modern system of values, and not simply with respect to the abolition of slavery. More broadly, this was the first step in replacing tribalism with the ideology of *gens una sumus*.

Modes of travel, however, had still hardly changed, which meant that first-hand experience of other cultures was just as limited for ordinary people. Only the soldiers and mariners who had gone on imperial seagoing expeditions into the previously unknown world were encountering cultures that they had never seen before. The Seven Years' War (1756–63) had taken British soldiers to France, but after their service on the European continent those soldiers went much further afield to secure colonies for the British. Some of those colonies had previously belonged to either France or Spain in the Americas, Africa, India, and the Caribbean. These ventures turned out to be important in many ways, the most obvious being that this accumulation of new territories made Britain the largest empire that the world had ever seen. The colonies of the British Empire were no longer limited to the cultures that had been found in the Age of Discovery; they now included even areas that had already been part of the known world, including India and parts of China. (Marco Polo had given accounts of both as early as 1300 AD.) In those countries, relationships that began only with trading concessions morphed in varying degrees into political control.

The overwhelming size of the British Empire has a special significance for our story. Just as British public opinion was both turning against slavery and slowly moving beyond tribal attitudes, a great deal of new territory was coming under British control. Sooner or later, the tension between these two apparently contradictory developments would become difficult to maintain. But for the moment, the rationale for empire—in a dangerous world, bigger is better—still seemed a powerful one.

Apprehensiveness about the aggressive intentions of other countries was still being reinforced by, for example, Napoleon's attempt to conquer the world in the first decade of the 19th century. Napoleon reminded all of Europe that one's neighbors were just as dangerous as they had ever been, and that, consequently, size still mattered. At this moment, the age-old threat of conquest by one's neighbors seemed no different to what it had always been. The 17th-century advance of the Ottoman armies into Europe still echoed as a frightening memory. The Ottoman Turks had been much feared for their habit of enslaving captives in war, Europeans included, and treating them brutally. Their advance had only been stopped at the eastern edge of Europe a century earlier.

And yet European attitudes toward other countries were slowly changing, and it was their attitude toward Turkey that illustrates the difference. During the 18th century, Europeans became fascinated with Turkish culture. For the first time, a serious number of people of one culture become entranced by another, contemporary culture. Unlike previous fascinations with ancient cultures, such as those of Greece and Rome, which were so far in the distant past that they were no longer a political or military threat, this was a European population idolizing a different nation that was still very much alive.

What had been happening for some time was that European seafarers had been spreading knowledge of and interest in other cultures by bringing back to Europe exotic items such as Turkish cloth and coffee, as well as Indian textiles and tea. Coffee and tea quickly became staples in Europe. These things were brought to a Europe that was slowly becoming both more affluent and more literate. It was affluent enough to indulge in unfamiliar goods, and literate enough to be able to create a shared opinion of them—a very public opinion, in this instance a widely shared enthusiasm for foreign cultures seen as intriguing and exotic. Mozart took part in the Turkish craze with his opera *Die Entführung aus dem Serail* (*The Abduction from the Seraglio*), and by incorporating Turkish elements in several of his other works. This was a case of a culture being charmed by another whose customs were remote from its own, and who were a terrifying presence not long ago. Similar enthusiasms were to follow: for example, the Japanese craze in 19th-century Britain that saw

W. S. Gilbert and Arthur Sullivan compose their wildly popular comic opera *The Mikado*. As time went on, similar enthusiasms would sweep across Europe. Travel might not have changed much by the time of the Turkish craze, but books, pamphlets, magazines, and newspapers could all feed this kind of interest.

In the long run, the greatest force for a change in attitudes toward other peoples would be this gradual rise of large reading publics, as other countries began to develop the levels of literacy that Britain had achieved. They, too, could then have the same kind of national conversations about moral issues through the medium of the printed word, thus developing an informed public opinion on questions of right and wrong in human life.

But a serious problem now came into view for the British. The Age of Discovery had led to a growth of empires, because in 1500 nobody had anything against empires. A larger and stronger country was safer in a dangerous world. The only difference between countries as far as empires were concerned was not that some countries deemed them morally acceptable and some didn't, but that some were able to create an empire, and some weren't. Yet by the late 18th century, the vigorous moral debate among the British reading public was beginning to complicate this way of thinking. Sooner or later, discussion of what was right and wrong in human affairs was bound to lead to thoughts about the liberty and equality of all peoples on earth, not just the Britishers who were taking part in the discussion.

As we've seen, standing athwart the progress of *gens una sumus* was an entrenched habit of taking people as they were when first encountered— that is, taking them to be defined only by their existing behaviors and customs. In 1741 David Hume began to undermine this attitude when he made a distinction between the potential that all human beings have, and the state that individuals or groups exist in because of their local circumstances. Hume observed "how nearly equal all men are in their bodily force, and even in their mental power and faculties, till cultivated by education."[1] Because this is a categorical assertion about the natural equality of all people, it is a roundabout assertion of the principle of *gens una sumus*. Every human being starts out in a state of near equality, and any later differences arise from his or her "education," which we can understand in a sense broader than simply one's schooling, taking it also to include any kind of socialization into the ways of a particular culture. Education, in this broader sense, is what separates different peoples. Peoples found in one state could have been otherwise if subjected to different kinds of cultural influences. But if it's only socialization that separates peoples, that raised a difficult question for the British. In Hume's account, all people are born "near equals." How could the colonizers justify their exerting power over peoples who were in principle their equals?

Daniel Hannan illuminates this contradiction from another direction, explaining that the British held the different nations of the British Isles together by attributing their union to a common set of political values. Rather than the English controlling the Welsh or the Scots by force, all were held together by the institutions to which each nation subscribed: "the sovereign parliament, the common law, secure property rights, an independent judiciary, etc." But, Hannan goes on, "If Britishness [as opposed to Englishness] was defined by equality before the law, representative government, property rights, and the rest, then as they became imperial subjects, the Jamaicans, Maltese, and Malayans must surely acquire a measure of them."[2] To return to Hume's observation: once shaped by the same education or socialization, all would have equal standing.

There is no doubt that the debate that took place within the British nation was beginning to affect its rationale for empire-building. Again, the impeachment of Warren Hastings, in which Edmund Burke accused Hastings of violating the rights of the Indian people, is powerful evidence of the change. It is hard to imagine, in an earlier time, a solemn parliamentary process in which a British official was accused of depriving a colonized peoples of their rights, because that very process suggests that the colonized should have the same rights that Englishmen enjoy.

Accordingly, the justification for England's holding so many countries in its power began to change. As the quest for empire began, Britain had been concerned to increase its strength and power so that it would not fall behind other European nations and find itself vulnerable to attack by a superior force. But as the new public opinion towards human equality developed, the rationale for Britain's controlling other peoples had to change. The idea that now came to the fore was that Britain had a responsibility towards those peoples: it would administer these territories for their own good. It could give them good governance at a stage in their development when they could not yet provide it for themselves. Isolation from the known world, (or in the case of India and China, remoteness from Europe, where modernity was already advancing rapidly) had left most of them far behind other cultures in their technological and economic development—in some cases, thousands of years behind. The responsibility of a benign British administration was therefore to help them to catch up. This idea gained currency in that familiar phrase, "The White Man's Burden."

Today, this is a much-derided idea, but its critics could not be more mistaken about what it really meant. It signaled one of the most important turning points in world history: it changed the rationale for empires, and in a way that would soon mean an end to those empires. It's a curious fact that the harshest critics of this idea ought to be the first to celebrate its importance in bringing about the result that they profess to want: namely, the abolition of empires.

That the cultures that had been either isolated from the known world's technological progress over thousands of years, or on its periphery, must sooner or later catch up was inevitable. The only questions were how long it would take, and how exactly it would happen. The spirit undergirding this later stage of the British Empire determined the answers to those questions. It would take place much more quickly, and with much less violence, simply because the philosophy of *gens una sumus* had begun to take hold in Britain in the 18th century.

In my book *Literature Lost* (1997), I discuss the change from the earlier to the later stages of imperialism: "Seen in historical context, colonialism is an intermediate stage between an unrestrained pressing of one's own claims without regard for those of others, and the final renunciation of those claims. A society that must convince itself that the occupation of another is for its own good is not too far away from accepting that it should not do so at all."[3]

Once this rationale is adopted, then, colonialism can't be more than a transitional phenomenon. It was, in fact, a half-way house on a long and

winding road. It was certainly better for all concerned than the early stages of empire had been, and it was bound to lead—after an intermediate
period of uncertain length—to full independence from colonial control.
In the beginning stages of European empires, European powers seized
control of territories far from home, because doing so made them secure
against competing powers. But in this second stage of imperialism the
British recognized the rights of their subjugated peoples and set out to
give them an efficient interim government that only an advanced society
was capable of administering. This would save the colonized peoples
from the chaos and internal conflict of lawlessness, and it would allow
them soon to enjoy an independent place in the modern world. Daniel
Hannan puts the matter thus: "British policy-makers during the 19th
century came to see their role as being based on stewardship. Once the
colonies reached the requisite level of political development, the aim
should be to oversee their development into sovereign allies." Hannan
calls this the British Empire's "self-dissolving quality, in that the political rights and values it disseminated tended to promote autonomy and
self-reliance." [4] This, whether stated openly or not, was the main rationale for colonial government by the 19th century, and it was an important step in the direction of *gens una sumus*. The heart of the matter was
not simply that Britain was introducing to its colonies forward-looking
innovations such as the rule of law and modern technology. The crucial
point was that Britain now regarded itself as responsible for the welfare
and development of the peoples of its empire.

In today's academia, the word "colonialism" is as bad as a four-letter
word: it's only used pejoratively. Colonialism is evil, with no ifs, ands,
or buts. When in 2017 Bruce Gilley wrote an article entitled "The Case
for Colonialism," the academic world virtually melted down. The journal that published it, *Third World Quarterly*, was compelled to retract the
article after petitions signed by thousands of professors demanded it do
so. Half the journal's editorial board had already resigned in protest, and
both its editor and the author received threats of violence. The criticisms
were of many kinds, but it was all too clear what the violent anger was
about. One of the intractable commandments of the present-day academic world states: thou shalt not say anything good about colonialism.

But this command can't be justified either as a statement of principle—ruling out any possibility of contrary evidence can never be a principle—or as a conclusion based in historical fact. The facts clearly don't support the position taken by Gilley's critics. Their position can therefore only be interpreted as an admission that scholarly analysis of history is not what matters to them; instead, their concerns begin and end with a radical political agenda. Real scholars weigh the facts, then commit themselves to an interpretation of them. Political activists invert that process: they commit in advance to an interpretation of history, and then refuse to look at facts that might invalidate their predetermined conclusion.

The radical critics were keeping their eyes firmly shut to a voluminous record of historical studies that examine how the advantages enjoyed by advanced societies are spread—sometimes by trade, sometimes by sheer propinquity, and sometimes by conquest. In the latter case the conqueror usually influences the conquered, but occasionally the influence moves in both directions. In the case of India, both the British and Indians influenced one another. These influences may be relatively minor—say, with respect to tastes in food or clothing—but they can also be fundamental to a society's organization. India now has a British-style democracy, British-style railways, a national language of English, and much more that derives from the erstwhile British stewardship.

Gilley's article took place within this once-thriving tradition of scholarship, but he added to that tradition the profoundly interesting idea that some degree of recolonization might now be beneficial to countries that have deteriorated to an appalling extent since the colonizers left. His analysis is thorough, informed, original, and thought-provoking. By contrast, his radical critics disgraced themselves and the institutions that had given them their academic appointments.[5] They were attempting to put an entire field of study off limits for scholarly investigation, lest it produce results that contradicted their ideology.

How successful were the British in undertaking this "stewardship," this good governance on behalf of peoples that they thought not yet ready to provide it for themselves? And—more relevant to my central concern—what impact did their efforts have on the development of relations between different peoples? Was the ideology of *gens una sumus* advanced by British colonial stewardship? Indeed, it was. For, however much the notions of colonial stewardship and good governance are now derided by radical scholars, they represented a giant step forward both for peoples that had lagged far behind the British in their development, and for the possibility of different peoples coexisting with a degree of mutual respect. For the first time on anything like this scale, peoples of different cultures now worked together and lived side by side, for the most part in relative harmony, and in pursuit of a common good. Individuals of different cultures were not just getting to know one another on a day-to-day basis, they were learning to accept one another as partners. It was an important beginning, one not to be derided merely because there was yet more work to be done before fully modern attitudes would be reached.

Conflict did, of course, occur from time to time, and it was sometimes bloody. But these relatively few violent episodes should not obscure the importance of what was happening. From the standpoint of the world's development, this late-colonial cooperation constituted a major advance. What radical critics always forget is that the relevant historical context for moral judgment is not that of the 21st century, but rather that of a slow progression beyond the attitudes of 1500. This second stage of Britain's colonial empire represented a major step beyond the outlook of that earlier era.

In a sense, the attitude of the Christian missionaries was now becoming public policy. Missionaries understood native people to be fellow human beings who had been held back by their cultures, isolated as they were from the advances made in the known world. They had been socialized in one way, but they could be just as easily socialized in another. A people in the stone age was not an inferior race, but one that needed to be brought into the modern era. Missionaries dedicated their lives to that task, and as such were pioneers of the philosophy of *gens una sumus.*

Did it all work? Did real comity between previously different peoples come about as a result? Did more understanding and good-will really develop among them? There is a great deal in the historical record that suggests that it did. This was, in fact, a breakthrough period in human history.

At its height, the British Empire included one quarter of the world's population, in territories that numbered nearly one hundred countries (the exact number depends on how one counts protectorates and the separate areas of what are now a single nation). But the population of Great Britain in the mid-19th century (the heyday of the British Empire) was only about twenty-seven million. The number that could be made available for duties in the Empire can only have been a very small proportion of the total. The number of British people in India, for example, was never more than a fraction of one percent of the Indian population. How could such a small number possibly have controlled about two hundred million people? The answer must surely be that British colonial rule was generally not felt to be onerous, and that it was even in some ways seen as benevolent. Many native peoples had already experienced other colonizers, and they preferred the British. The reason for this is obvious: only Britain had had that extensive 18th-century public conversation about morality, one that touched on the rights of all mankind, including those of colonized peoples.

The decline of the British Empire tells the same story. While that empire no longer exists as it did at its height, it's remarkable that still in 2022 there were fourteen countries that voluntarily acknowledged Queen Elizabeth II as their head of state, and fifty-four that belonged to a commonwealth of nations based on their former status as British colonies. All of this would hardly have been possible if the relationship between the British administrators and the peoples they administered had simply been one of hated overseers and resentful captives. We might well ask: did any other empire in world history ever end in this way? And the answer is clear: there never was a comparable case. An attempt to create a French union of a similar kind failed. Former French colonies wanted rid of France, period.

The readiness of British colonies to fight with their colonizers in the two World Wars tells the same story. These were, after all, occasions when the British had their hands full fighting other European powers, and when the colonized peoples could easily have expelled their colonial ruler. But they did not. Instead, they fought on the side of the British, conscious of the fact that they were far better off with them than without them. And they fought well: the forty battalions of the Indian Gurkhas were among the most feared soldiers of the Second World War.

In the First World War, a surprising proportion of the Empire's forces in France at the outset of the war were Indian: about a third. The total of Indian troops who served in Europe during that war exceeded one million. No less an authority than Field-Marshal Sir Claude Auchinleck, Commander-in-Chief of the Indian Army from 1942, judged that the British "couldn't have come through both wars if they hadn't had the Indian Army."[6] Winston Churchill paid tribute to "The unsurpassed bravery of Indian soldiers and officers."[7]

Another telling indicator can be seen in the present-day reach of two favorite sports of the British: cricket and rugby. These two sports thrive only in former British colonies. Probably more than anything else, cricket ties India, Pakistan, and the West Indies to England. Those countries are all crazy about cricket, which would scarcely have been possible had there not been a certain amount of affection among the colonized for the British. That affection went both ways: the great Indian cricketer Kumar Shri Ranjitsinhji played in England in the late 19th and early 20th centuries, and his forceful yet wonderfully elegant play caused a sensation. He was the first batsman ever to score more than three thousand runs in a season of English first class cricket. The Manchester Guardian's greatly respected cricket correspondent Neville Cardus called him "the Midsummer Night's Dream of cricket." Ranji (as he was popularly known) not only played cricket in England, he played for England—that is, for the national team. He is remembered as one of the greatest batsmen of all time. His nephew Kumar Shri Duleepsinhji essentially repeated his uncle's cricketing career, also playing for England with great success. They are legends of Britain's favorite game—for the English just as they are for the Indians. Gens una sumus made serious progress with Ranji and Duleep.

The education of Indians in the colonial period tells a similar story. Well-to-do Indian families sent their children to get an education in England, while less affluent ones sent their children to English-language schools. But education of Indians didn't stop at elementary and secondary schools. Already in the 19th century, higher education was being provided for large numbers of Indian students. When Indian leaders began to agitate for independence from Britain, it was all too obvious that those leaders had been British-trained and were using British ideas and arguments to argue for their independence. They were just as much intellectual children of the 18th-century debate in England as the British themselves. Mohandas Ghandi trained for the law at the Inner Temple in London, and Jawarharlal Nehru was educated at Harrow School (as was Winston Churchill) and Trinity College, Cambridge. Several of the post-independence leaders of African countries also studied at British universities: Seretse Khama, the first President of Botswana, studied at Balliol College, Oxford, and at the Inner Temple in London; Kwame Nkrumah, the first Prime Minister of Ghana, studied at the London School of Economics, University College, London, and at Gray's Inn; and Hastings Banda, the first President of Malawi, studied at the University of Edinburgh.

During the first World War, Gandhi wrote: "I discovered the British Empire had certain ideas with which I had fallen in love, and one of those ideas is that every subject of the British Empire has the freest scope for his energies and efforts."[8] In Gandhi's case, Britain had certainly succeeded in preparing an Indian for self-government.

Another compelling source of evidence that the British prepared their colonies for independence in a way that other empires did not can be seen in the record of what has happened since independence. There is a marked difference between those decolonized territories that were part of the British Empire, and those that were not. Niall Ferguson cites the conclusions of the great political scientist Seymour Martin Lipset: "...countries that were former British colonies had a significantly better chance of achieving enduring democratization after independence than those ruled by other countries."[9] It's not hard to see why: the British brought to their colonies the administrative structures and institutions that were part of their own experience with democracy, and this at a time when some of the other colonial powers of Europe were themselves not yet democracies. After independence, British-style institutions were adopted by many of the newly independent peoples.

My own personal experience adds some detail to this general picture. My family is linked by marriage to that of an Indian engineer. As the families got to know each other better, I was surprised to learn how much of my education was familiar to my new Indian relatives. We had even read many of the same children's books.

All of this suggests that the British did indeed provide good steward-ship much of the time. They provided a regime of law and order that put an end to what had been constant tribal massacres. They provided modern courts that adjudicated disputes fairly—disputes that might otherwise have escalated to extensive inter-tribal violence. They institut-ed schools that prepared the children of the colonized to take part in the governance of their country. They introduced better farming methods. They brought the manufacturing capabilities of the Industrial Revolution that the British had initiated, and that brought with it economic devel-opment and advancement. They built roads, railways, and ports. They did their best to stamp out slavery, cannibalism, and euthanasia of the disabled or the elderly where these things had long been the custom. They reined in the brutality of tribal leaders. Even in India, a civilized nation with a long written history, the cruel custom of suttee, in which a widow was burned to death on her dead husband's funeral pyre, was outlawed by the British—much to the relief of many Indians.

Bruce Gilley cites more evidence of the degree to which the colonized had come to work with their colonizers to construct for themselves a better life: "Millions of people moved closer to areas of more intensive colonial rule, sent their children to colonial schools and hospitals, went beyond the call of duty in positions in colonial governments, reported crimes to colonial police, migrated from non-colonized to colonized areas, fought for colonial armies, and participated in colonial political processes—all relatively voluntary acts."[10] Gilley also points to cases where colonized peoples clearly showed a preference for colonial rule because they knew that the alternative was government by enemy war-lords, whom they feared.[11] He summarizes that colonialism "led to im-provements in living conditions for most Third World peoples during most episodes of Western colonialism."[12]

How very different this was from the way in which other imperial re-gimes treated their colonized peoples. Belgium's King Leopold II was notorious for his brutality towards the African people under his control. To this day, Russians who are trying to recreate the greater Russian Empire treat Ukrainians as nothing more than an impediment to the augmentation of their empire. Ukrainians have been raped, tortured, kidnapped, and executed. For the Japanese rulers who were intent on enlarging their empire before and during the Second World War, only land mattered—not the Chinese people. The 1937 Rape of Nanjing is one of the most brutal episodes in world history. Japanese soldiers murdered at least two hundred thousand Chinese civilians and committed at least twenty thousand rapes.[13] It was no wonder that the peoples of British colonies usually didn't revolt: they knew that their present circumstances were much better than the possible alternatives.

To anyone who is prepared to look with an unbiased eye at the historical record, there can be little doubt that British colonialism was, on balance, a positive force, and remarkably benign when compared to its colonial predecessors and contemporaries. But from our point of view, what is most important is that this late stage of British colonialism was probably the most important and forward-looking way-station on the road to the modern consensus of *gens una sumus*. Very different peoples were living side by side, working with and for one another, relying on one another and having some regard for one another, on a scale for which there was no precedent. This was surely one of the most important factors in the gradual eclipse of the tribal world of 1500.

What happened when British colonialism ended shortly after World War II provides even more compelling evidence as to its relatively benevolent character. Once former European colonies were left to themselves, the older tribalism reasserted itself in far too many cases. This resulted often in bloody tribal wars. In Africa especially, the wars that the colonizers had so long prevented broke out again almost as soon as the colonial regimes ended.

In *Literature Lost*, I cite a summary of what had happened in the decades following the end of the colonial era:

> In Nigeria, whole populations of the Ibo have been annihilated by rival tribes. Civil war in Ethiopia has produced horrendous numbers of dead. In Mozambique, the number who have died in the civil war that has been going on since 1975 approaches one million. In Somalia, tribal warlords have been using mass starvation to improve their own tribe's position. In Rwanda

the war of extermination between the Hutu and the Tutsi tribes
has claimed at least half a million lives. A ferocious racial war
has broken out in Sri Lanka between Tamils and Sinhalese, in
which "tens of thousands of people were massacred in the most
gruesome way . . . ." In Timor, up to two hundred thousand East
Timorese have been killed by Indonesians or starved to death by
famine since 1975.[14]

The list of cases cited here could have been multiplied. In a section of his
article headed "The Costs of Anti-Colonialism," Gilley gives further examples, estimating that, of eighty countries which decolonized, at least
half experienced domestic chaos and trauma.[15] These countries all re-
verted to their former practices of tribalism and political tyranny, though
often under the banner of a modern label borrowed from Europeans:
communism. But there was really nothing new about what they were doing. The ideology of communism was just a convenient cover to revert to
age-old forms of dictatorship and tyranny. However politically incorrect
it may be to say so, the end of the colonial period meant a severe setback
for the progress of *gens una sumus*. Old-style racism came back with a ven-
geance. That we are all one people is the most anti-racist idea in world
history, and colonial stewardship was a crucial force in promoting it.
For anyone who genuinely cares about the progress of anti-racism—real
anti-racism, not the phony and deeply racist version of it now peddled by
race-hustling charlatans like Ibram Kendi—the colonial period ended
too soon. When it ended, tribalism (which is to say, racism) returned in
full force.

The plain fact is that the organized promotion of *gens una sumus* was
the legacy of the British Enlightenment. The British Empire was a powerful force in its promotion, but the idea needed to be nurtured in the
colonies for longer than it actually was. As a result, these territories paid
a dreadful price for their premature decolonization, which permitted the
return of vicious forms of tribalism. There was a literal price to be paid,
too. For the most part, the wealth gap between the developed world and
recently decolonized countries *grew* after decolonization, where it had
been declining before independence. Niall Ferguson is undoubtedly

correct when he says that "the notion that British imperialism tended to impoverish colonized countries seems inherently problematic.... It has been since independence that the [economic] gap between the colonizer and the ex-colony has become a gulf."[16] An illustrative example is that British per capita GDP was seven times that of Zambia in 1955, but by 2002 it was twenty-eight times Zambian per capita GDP.

To say this is not to deny that among the colonists were some who displayed the same failings that any group of human beings always exhibits. Military commanders sometimes overreacted to local disturbances and killed wantonly when a milder response would have sufficed. But these excesses were not typical, and they never came close to the level of brutality that was routine in other empires—for example, the Japanese or Ottoman empires. Though some administrators were greedy and corrupt, many others regarded colonial service as a calling and prided themselves on honest government. That was certainly what the British government expected of them. Edgar Wallace's "Sanders of the River" is doubtless an idealized figure of a wise and just colonial administrator, yet he is not simply a fictional creation. Just as we see in Wallace's books, the British really did suppress tribal wars, providing a stability that was conspicuously absent after their departure.

There is one final point that must be made concerning the end of the British Empire. Empires had been a worldwide phenomenon throughout history, and they are now (almost) a thing of the past. What is unique about the British Empire is not that the British (like hundreds of other peoples) built an empire, but that by peacefully relinquishing that empire they brought the era of empires to a close. That considerable achievement still goes largely unrecognized. To sharpen the point: the most effective anti-imperialists in world history were the later British imperialists. They dismantled the imperialism that had been so prominent a part of human life for thousands of years.

Regardless of this well-documented fact, it's largely the British Empire that attracts the attention and the scorn of radicals. The attacks on Bruce Gilley's essay demonstrated an unwillingness even to consider that the British Empire might have had some positive features. One obvious blind spot in the radicals' outlook is their failure to ponder why this was the last of the great empires. Throughout history there had been hundreds of unapologetic empires that never doubted their own legitimacy, ending only through dissolution and military defeat. In their place, newer empires then arose. Only the British Empire dissolved itself, and in doing so bequeathed to the world the conviction that empires cannot be justified. If they had anything like an adequate grasp of human history, these anti-imperialists would be celebrating the British Empire. Only Britain's example created the present worldwide consensus that imperialism is no longer permissible. Many countries now oppose Russia's attempted imperial conquest of Ukraine, but they do so not because they are sympathetic to Ukraine and hostile to Russia. Their concern is to protect and preserve the international consensus on imperialism that the British created by their example.

Modern radical scholars like to say that "Whiteness" is the main obstacle to racial justice, while claiming that they are the true anti-racists. But racism is not something that was invented by a particular race: it was the universal norm until something happened to change it. And the historical record shows that the greatest single step forward in overcoming racism was taken by the British, as their attitudes to empire changed. Anti-racism was their innovation. Modern radical activists, of whatever ethnicity, are working within the tradition of a value system—*gens una sumus*—initiated and developed precisely by those they vilify.

The sheer size of the British Empire underlines its importance in the spread of the idea of *gens una sumus*. The original breeding ground of this ideology was, as we've seen, 17th- and 18th-century Britain, but as the Empire grew to cover a quarter of the globe, Britons spread *gens una sumus* throughout that domain. And yet, important as this development was for our progress toward modern racial attitudes, it was still to be outshone by arguably the greatest of all the forces that have made for the near-universal acceptance of *gens una sumus*. That force was the creation of a universal modern civilization, which was, once more, for the most part the work of the English-speaking world. How that came about is the subject of the next chapter.

Chapter Five: Modernity
Spreads Humane Values

W E'VE SEEN THAT the world of 1500 was one of almost total ignorance of peoples other than an individual's own, and that a general apprehensiveness about the unknown was often raised to the level of
hatred by raiding and warfare; that peoples at extremely different levels
of development confronted each other for the first time during the Age
of Discovery, thus laying the groundwork for a number of multi-racial
societies; that the growth of the reading public in Britain led to a vibrant
public discussion of moral questions and ideas, particularly those concerning human equality and slavery, which allowed informed public
opinion to become a serious force in human affairs, a consequence being
the abolition of slavery; and that later stages of colonialism saw people
of different races living and working together on a scale never previously
seen. For the first time, one people felt that it was responsible for the
well-being of another.

With all of this, a large part of the world was unmistakably moving in
the direction of *gens una sumus*. The British were already spreading the
idea throughout their enormous empire, but a new force with an even
greater reach was about to disseminate it even more broadly. This was
the long and complex technological revolution that began in the English-
speaking world around the year 1800. It would gradually spread to the
rest of the world, but it would be a stronger force in the Anglosphere than
elsewhere for a long time to come. By comparison with this new development, previous innovations in human life, such as that of agriculture or
the wheel, had had far more circumscribed effects. In those cases, access
to food became more reliable, moving things from one place to another
became easier, and some limited kinds of machinery were made possible.
But this new technological advance in human life was so overwhelming
in its effects that it has resulted in a universal civilization, a way of life
whose main elements are now common to most people in the world.

The cumulative impact on humanity of this universal civilization as it
spread from its mainly English-speaking progenitors to the rest of the

world has been astonishing. It has brought about the most complete transformation of human life we have ever seen. Average life spans have more than doubled, diseases that once devastated entire countries have been tamed, populations that were consistently on the verge of severe hunger are now adequately fed, and in many areas of the world economies are so strong that large numbers of people live as only a privileged few once did. Literacy has spread throughout the world, and even peoples who had been isolated before 1500 are gradually being drawn into the advanced culture that had developed in the Anglosphere. It has always been true that advanced cultures transmitted useful knowledge and innovations to others, whether through conquest or trade, but the scale of transformation brought about by this new universal civilization goes well beyond anything in history. The entire world has been swept up in a new mode of living, based on technological and scientific innovations that have been shared worldwide. The cumulative effect of these innovations amounts to nothing less than the development of modernity.

The British Empire had spread the values of the British Enlightenment across the empire, but the universal civilization that resulted from its technological revolution spread those values even further. This is therefore how that crucial modern idea of a common humanity circulated throughout the world, the idea that is invoked whenever anyone accuses another of racism. It's not an idea native to Africa, or Asia, or the Americas. It arose in the Anglosphere and was spread only as the reach of the Anglosphere increased by two distinct waves: empire, and technological revolution.

How did this technological revolution begin, and how did it then develop? The ultimate origins of this extraordinary development must be sought in a series of seminal events that shaped British history and created a greater degree of freedom for British subjects than existed anywhere else. What began with Magna Carta developed steadily through many subsequent episodes: Simon de Montfort's summoning of a parliament in 1265; the separation of the Church of England from the Roman Catholic Church (in effect, a proto-Brexit); the civil war that institutionalized the primacy of Parliament; the Glorious Revolution of 1688–89; and, finally, the Enlightenment.

There is a familiar phrase that sums up English freedom: "An Englishman's home is his castle." The broadening of individual liberty freed gifted individuals to think productively and to act on the results of their thought. Thinking and learning naturally led to innovation. An early consequence was that even before the start of the Industrial Revolution, Britain was already the world's leading commercial power.

The long revolution that gave us modernity began at the end of the 18th century in England with what is known as the Industrial Revolution—the invention and application of machinery to the production of goods. For centuries the conditions of human life had changed relatively little, but now scientific and technological innovation went into high gear. Yet what was set in motion was much more than any specific innovation: the Industrial Revolution was really a cascading series of inventions, in which one innovation led to the next, and then the next again. In short, what had really happened was not some particular inventions, but the beginning of a habit of invention. The result was a never-ending sequence that has already lasted two hundred years, and it has profoundly changed life everywhere.

It's not difficult to see how this worked. The first large-scale harnessing of technology to manufacture a few specific goods produced them in such quantities that their cost was greatly reduced. However, once that initial manufacturing improvement had taken place, it was inevitable not only that people would look for even better ways to manufacture those same goods, but also that they would try to use similar technologies to manufacture other goods with the same kind of efficiency. In effect, the Industrial Revolution ushered in a permanent search not just for better ways of manufacturing goods, but for better ways of doing anything and everything, one that continues to this day.

Sooner or later, this revolution was bound to lead not just to better ways of producing known goods, but to the creation of goods that had never been imagined before. Bicycles and radios were not just better versions of existing goods—they were unique new commodities. The refinement and improvement of the means of production never stopped, which meant that goods became ever better and cheaper. Living standards thus began to rise, and they kept rising, year by year. One generation always lived better than its predecessor. All these improvements were, of course, eagerly adopted outside England; it was the global spread of this culture of innovation that initiated a universal civilization, an increasingly uniform modern way of life. Some countries followed more quickly than others, but eventually almost everyone came along.

Take, for example, the difference between England and Nigeria two hundred years ago, and the difference now. Two hundred years ago, a visitor to both countries would have seen two completely different situations and two totally different ways of life. Today, however, in both countries he would see streets with automobiles; airports with planes; homes with telephones, refrigerators, and televisions; soldiers in uniforms that look rather alike; police with very similar duties; and so on. Even dress is standardizing on Anglosphere models. Chinese President Xi Jinping often wears the Western suit and tie, as do many dignitaries at the United Nations.

As this constant dynamic of technological innovation spread worldwide, the value system that gave rise to that dynamic tended to spread with it. But there were more specific ways in which northern European technology promoted a sense of a common humanity. The technological revolution soon removed the physical barriers that had stood in the way of people from one culture meeting those of another.

Three British engineers gave us steam-powered travel. After James Watt had invented the steam engine, in the late 1830s Isambard Kingdom Brunel adapted Watt's engine to ships, and Richard Trevithick adapted it to rail locomotives. Railroads developed with astonishing rapidity in England: within a few decades giant railway stations were being built on all sides of London. For the first time, ordinary people could now travel hundreds of miles easily and cheaply.

Because the Industrial Revolution set in motion a whole culture of technological innovation, it was inevitable that engineers everywhere would always be looking at existing machinery and thinking of ways to improve on it. This made it inevitable that they would try to find an engine even better than the steam engine. And they found one: the internal combustion engine, which developed in the late 19th century from the cumulative efforts of several northern European and American engineers.

With American mass production, automobiles were made available to the public in the first few years of the 20th century. That meant another giant leap forward in travel: whereas locomotives restricted travelers to the set routes of the railroad, automobiles freed people to determine their own routes.

The culture of engineering innovation in travel would not stop with the automobile. In 1903, two American engineers, the Wright brothers, decided to go one better, with travel by air. The speed of aviation's refinement and its adoption for general use is astonishing when compared to the progress of earlier technologies. Airplanes were already a major factor in the First World War, just a decade after the first flight.

These developments revolutionized travel and thus greatly reduced the physical barrier of distance between different peoples. Even so, none of this would have made much difference if ordinary people had been no better off economically than they were in 1500. But the technological revolution also improved their economic well-being as goods and services became progressively cheaper. Trains made the distribution of food far more efficient: they ran through the night to the major London railway stations, carrying huge quantities of food from the surrounding counties for distribution to shopkeepers throughout the London area each morning. This lowered costs and left everyone better off. Widespread use of the automobile facilitated the rise of supermarkets that lowered food costs still more, leading to even greater economic well-being. As living standards kept rising, tourism was at last no longer restricted to the wealthy. More and more people were becoming acquainted with other peoples, and with this new knowledge the older suspicion of other cultures began to be replaced by curiosity and wonder. The impact on human life of the always increasing stream of new technologies that were set in motion by the Industrial Revolution is incalculable.

One innovation is particularly relevant to our story: the harnessing of electricity. This led to a series of inventions that greatly increased everyone's knowledge of the world beyond their own culture. Radio, television, films, the internet—all these highly important means of communication were made possible by electrical energy. Today, they disseminate knowledge of the world at all hours of the day. The ignorance of the rest of the world that was near universal in the year 1500 has now been displaced by a constant stream of information.

But electrical energy did much more than transmit knowledge of the world—it also accelerated the culture of innovation and change, and with it the progress of the new universal civilization. After a relatively brief period in which gas lights were used in houses, electricity began to be used for domestic lighting in the 1880s. Both were strong factors in the promotion of reading, and more reading meant more dissemination of knowledge of all kinds, including knowledge of the world. Once again, Britain led the way: the Edison Electric Light Station, built in London at the Holborn Viaduct, was the world's first coal-fired power station generating electricity for public use.

The steadily increasing momentum of innovation meant a constant stream of new machines of every conceivable kind and for every conceivable purpose. Refrigeration meant a major improvement in the storage and preservation of food; this, together with a series of popular kitchen devices, has created a universal kitchen culture. Whatever human beings had been doing before the Industrial Revolution, the new culture of engineering innovation would sooner or later turn up better ways of doing it, and then spread them rapidly across the world.

Take farm machinery: Americans, confronted with very large areas to cultivate and an inadequate supply of manpower, set about inventing machines that would automate agricultural production. These inventions spread across the globe, and soon enough farming throughout the world became far more efficient and productive than it had ever been. This machinery, too, is now part of the developing universal civilization that has raised living standards everywhere while spreading modern values.

The highly sophisticated modern medicine we enjoy today is another result of the British Industrial Revolution. It too developed out of that culture of technological and scientific innovation. Once more, while the first major advances were made in Northern Europe and America, modern medicine's benefits soon began to spread. Life-spans increased dramatically, first in Europe and America, then (albeit more slowly) across the globe. Hospitals that practice Western medicine are now found all over the world. These advances in medicine, agriculture, and travel were of course frequently brought by colonial powers to the peoples they colonized.

To appreciate just how astonishing the arrival and impact of this worldwide technological revolution has been, we have only to compare it to other major innovations that changed life in the past—that is, to those occasions in human history where innovations were sufficiently important to spread quickly around the known world, from one culture to another. Key innovations like the wheel, writing, agriculture, and durable building construction arise seemingly at random. It would be hard to explain why agriculture developed where and when it did; likewise the wheel, or permanent buildings made of stone. Particular people developed these processes, innovations, and customs, and they were found to be so useful that they spread throughout the contiguous cultures of the known world.

Mesopotamia already had stone buildings, agriculture, the wheel, writing, even a written governmental code (the code of Hammurabi), but the actual origins of these innovations are hard to pin down. It's possible that the Mesopotamians themselves originated some of them. It's therefore natural to ask: why the Mesopotamians? A mild climate and fruitful terrain may be a partial explanation, but chance is likely the more important factor.

Some of the innovations of classical antiquity were more complex. Over and above its more specific fruits of thought, Athens gave us the idea that it was important to think, and to think deeply, about everything and anything. What the Greeks really taught us was to use our brains. The Romans mainly applied that lesson to large-scale administrative organization, the result being one of the best organized and most durable empires the world had ever seen. Why the Greeks and why the Romans rather than the Germans or the Celts? Who knows. All we can say is that advances seem often to come from places that show some obvious geographical advantages, but that chance always looms large. Gifted individuals are as unpredictable in history as they are crucial.

When compared to any of these innovations, the revolution in human life that began in England around 1800 is extraordinary in so many ways. First, this was not one innovation or discovery, but rather an entire culture of innovation that continues to this day, two centuries later. The Industrial Revolution was the beginning of a never-ending revolution.

But a second (and more important) reason the Industrial Revolution isn't like past innovations in human life is that it's possible to identify why it began when and where it did. The Industrial Revolution was the logical outgrowth of a political tradition that had given Britons more freedom than any other European society. This tradition led to growing affluence, to widening literacy, and finally to the culture of innovation that set off the worldwide technological revolution and its associated universal civilization.

We can therefore say with certainty that the British political soil from which it arose was the decisive factor in the development of the technological revolution. Some lesser factors may certainly have helped: the severe winters of northern Europe certainly encouraged ingenious adaptations and technological advances that would increase the chance of survival in a challenging climate. Even so, the northerly location of Britain was clearly less important than the social and political environment when it came to driving innovation there.

The value system of *gens una sumus* that spread with this universal modern civilization doesn't yet prevail everywhere. Much of the Middle East is still riven with racial and religious hatreds. Yet even there, it's possible to see more modern attitudes developing. For example, the Iranian people are obviously not happy with a government that has its roots in medieval attitudes. But what's clear is that most modern people's sense of belonging to a common humanity was birthed by the British Enlightenment's commitment to *gens una sumus*, and spread by means of the technological revolution.

The English language, too, helped to spread this value system. English is now the acknowledged international language, and—which almost amounts to the same thing—the language of the internet. In many countries of the world, particularly the Scandinavian countries, English has almost achieved the status of a second national language, with most people effectively bilingual. At various times in the past there have been examples of a *lingua franca* that was either global in its scope or at least viable throughout a cluster of contiguous cultures. In the

Middle Ages and into the beginning of the modern era, scholars in different countries spoke to each other in Latin. In 1687, Isaac Newton was still using Latin for his great work *Philosophiae Naturalis Principia Mathematica*. After the use of Latin declined, East European scholars would talk to each other in German. In the 19th century it seemed that French would become the international language, and in 1919 the two languages of the League of Nations were French and English. But by the time the United Nations was founded after the Second World War, the working documents of the UN were all in English. The internet has now made English a *lingua franca* whose reach and dominance exceeds that of any of its predecessors by a wide margin.

It is in large part because of the spread of this universal civilization that racism has receded, after having been a staple of the world for nearly all of human history. The world now contains many societies in which people of different races intermingle as valued colleagues, admired public figures, and trusted friends and family. The sense of interracial togetherness now goes well beyond the superficial goodwill caused by widespread tourism.

And so *gens una sumus*—raised to the level of a social philosophy in the English-speaking world, then spread by its empire and by its powerful and ongoing technological revolution—at last came to predominate in world affairs. But let's note once more that while *gens una sumus* is universally accepted in theory, the practical reality is not nearly the same. It's now an orthodoxy, but it's in the nature of orthodoxies that lip service is often paid to them while they are actually being ignored. There are still all too many situations worldwide and even within the Anglosphere itself where a professed allegiance to *gens una sumus* is, in practice, a cover for a virulent racism that issues in spiteful criticisms of certain groups—including, now, even the population group that first promoted that idea.

It seems safe to say that just as critical innovations in human life have come from all kinds of different cultures over thousands of years, we can expect more innovations in the future, in places we can't possibly predict, from peoples whose identities we could not possibly now guess, and for reasons of which we are still completely innocent. But we can hazard a guess that the period of innovation that we have now lived with for some two hundred years will always be far and away the most important of them all.

My last chapter is devoted to the many misconceptions to which an ignorance of the origin and development of *gens una sumus* gives rise.

Chapter Six: Damaging Myths and Delusions

THE PRECEDING CHAPTERS aimed to explain just how the world changed over the last five hundred years in one profoundly important respect. Starting off from a climate of apprehensiveness and even outright hostility between peoples and nations, we have moved to a sense of the commonality of all human beings. And we have done so not through a gradual and universal drift in that direction, but rather because of specific events and developments that happened at particular times and places. Foremost among them was certainly the vibrant public debate that had developed in Britain with the spread of literacy, and the subsequent spread of the resulting ideas around the world, first through the reach of the British Empire, and then by the power of its technological revolution.

These conclusions are not simply a matter of historical interest. If valid, they would, or at least should, completely change the understanding of many of the most hotly disputed issues of our time. In fact, my conclusions are completely at variance with many ideas that now have a considerable following. If I am correct, those latter ideas are demonstrably wrong because rooted in a serious misunderstanding of how the modern world came to the idea of our common humanity—to *gens una sumus*. The most important part of that misunderstanding concerns the people who brought about this monumental change.

The bad ideas I am talking about are not simply intellectual mistakes, but rather dangerous delusions that fuel some of the most destructive currents in modern political and social life. They are so insidious that they undermine the health of our society. They corrupt university curricula and interfere with free speech and inquiry on college campuses; they damage our children's education in the schools; they interfere with professional training and competence; they do untold damage to the progress of minorities, especially of African-Americans; they poison the political atmosphere; and they were even the ultimate cause of the recent undermining and defunding of many American police forces, and thus of the recent dramatic increase in violent crime in many parts of the country.

Let's take these delusions one by one. The first is the claim that we are threatened by a widespread ideology of arrogant White supremacy, and by unearned White privilege. Whites have relative economic prosperity, it is said, only because they have stolen it from others. They illegitimately occupy almost all leadership and managerial posts in our society and elbow aside members of other groups who ought to have had their share of such positions. This allegedly damages minorities in a variety of ways, and because of this, White people are uniquely responsible for their disadvantaged status.[1]

There are two distinct parts to this complaint: one has to do with the advantages that Whites enjoy, the other with White attitudes to other races. As to the first of these: in the preceding chapter I showed how the amazing transformation of human life during the last two hundred years has been due mainly to the culture of innovation that arose in Britain and its North American offshoot, the United States. That fact must be the cornerstone of any well-informed judgment of the reasons both for relative White prosperity and for White prominence in educational curricula. It makes no sense to complain about the prominence of a specific group of people in modern life, if the form that modernity has taken was determined by the enormous and highly complex leap forward taken by those very people.

The far-reaching changes in human life that constitute modernity had to begin somewhere. It did so among a particular group of Europeans and their North American cousins. Individual strands that fed into it came from other times and places, but the Anglosphere was where everything suddenly came together, setting in motion the most profound changes in human life that we have ever seen. Because those changes started and developed largely in the English-speaking world, that society naturally enjoyed its benefits first. How could that possibly have been otherwise? As they invented modernity, their economic and political development surged ahead of that of other peoples. If, say, Africans had invented modernity, they would likewise have surged ahead of everyone else. But they didn't. Some of that initial advantage lingers today, both in European societies and in people of European descent, because the improved circumstances of earlier generations were inevitably passed down to succeeding ones. But this has nothing to do with an illegitimate "White privilege." The people who invent something naturally use it before anyone else!

Since White Europeans effected these profound changes, it can never be said that they stole the resultant benefits away from minorities or anyone else, as Critical Race Theory (CRT) would have us believe.[2] What really happened was the reverse: Europeans created those innovations and gave them to everyone else, including minorities. Every time that any member of a people that was not among the Anglosphere's innovators and inventors uses a phone, drives a car, goes to an expertly trained doctor, consults the internet, flies or travels by rail to vacation in a foreign country, reads a newspaper, watches television, pays his mortgage, eats refrigerated food that is reliably in first-rate condition—and we could extend this list forever—he is benefiting from the initiative and hard work of the people who gave all of this to us. These are just some of the hallmarks of our modern way of life, of modernity. We should be grateful to those who gave us our good health, our greater longevity, our prosperity, and so much besides. Yet radical ideologues instead complain about the very population group that made these things available.

Politically correct radicals are always on the lookout for trivial instances of "cultural appropriation," such as when Europeans wear non-Western items of clothing. But they are curiously blind to where their misguided logic must lead, for they themselves routinely commit cultural appropriation on a scale that dwarfs anything they condemn. I mentioned above a long list of the things that the Anglosphere made possible for the rest of the world. Using the paranoid logic of the radical Left, we could justifiably say that people of color have culturally appropriated every one of those things. When they do something as simple as switching on an electric light or riding in a car, they are appropriating the culture of European innovators. Two simple facts ought to put an end to the complaints: first, nearly everyone on earth has benefited from the two-centuries-long technological and scientific revolution in the Anglosphere that gave us modernity; second, nobody from the Anglosphere begrudges its being enjoyed (or "appropriated") by people of other cultures.

Just as complaints about White privilege rest on an ignorance of modern history, so the complaints about White racism and White supremacy result from a failure to understand how modern racial attitudes developed. When radicals accuse all Whites of racism, they are committing themselves to an anti-racist way of thinking—that is, to the ideology of *gens una sumus*—that was in fact developed by those same people whom they single out. We need only ask: where was the African or Asian movement that developed or promoted a philosophy of *gens una sumus*? It is a fact of history that while the British were developing this anti-racist ideology, racism was ubiquitous beyond their sphere of influence.

Radical activists deliberately minimize the enormous progress that the United States has made with respect to race relations, yet it's clear to any unbiased observer that they are now infinitely better than they were in 1950. Radicals who tell us that there has been no progress during this time are not just ignoring that progress, they are actively trying to sabotage it by stoking racial animosity. Racial strife is far too useful a weapon in their war against capitalism for them to accept the plain fact that racism has long been on the decline. Radical social transformation can only be sold to an unhappy society as the relief from that unhappiness.

Ibram X. Kendi often insists that anti-racism and anti-capitalism are inextricably linked: according to Kendi, a person cannot be anti-racist and pro–free market.[3] History teaches exactly the opposite lesson. The modern philosophy of *gens una sumus*—the genuine anti-racism of modernity—developed in the literate culture of 17th- and 18th-century Britain that resulted from the prosperity generated by its relatively free markets. Kendi has things backwards. It's capitalism, not anti-capitalism, that is required for anti-racism to thrive. For Kendi and for others like him, anti-racism is a convenient, though dishonest, vehicle for their Marxist ambitions.

The second major misconception consists in a misunderstanding of the status of our modern ideology of *gens una sumus*. Radicals think that it's a value system that is timeless and permanent—it's simply the natural state of affairs in human life. In their view, therefore, it can be used to judge anyone of any period, because it must have reigned at any time and in any place. They also imagine that they are the only perfect exemplars of this anti-racist ideology—that they own it, and can judge everyone else, in varying degrees, as falling short. Ibram Kendi even seems to believe that nobody really understood what anti-racism is until he explained it to us.

The truth, as we've seen, is the exact opposite of these claims. First, *gens una sumus* is a product of modernity; just a few centuries ago, it barely existed anywhere. Second, it's not a natural frame of mind, but rather a system of thought that had to be developed, maintained, and even fought for. Third, though *gens una sumus* belongs to us all, if we must single out any group that pioneered its development and ensured its acceptance, it would certainly not be the leftist radicals and ethnocentric ideologues of the modern era. The group of people that first propounded it, developed it, and fought for it were neither radicals nor minorities, but rather the British people of the 18th century. Its triumph was the achievement of the British Enlightenment, and those places in the modern world that are still strangers to it are precisely the places where the influence of the Enlightenment is weakest. It is a credo that rose to a dominant position in world affairs first by spreading throughout the British Empire, and later as a concomitant of the modernity that overtook the world having begun with the Industrial Revolution. Today's radicals are really laggards with respect to this revolutionary idea, yet they condemn its pioneers.

In this book I've tried to tell the story of the progress of *gens una sumus*. It's a fine story, a story of how the modern world was created out of a much less happy one. The people who made that story happen are genuinely its heroes, and they should be our heroes. Their triumph was noble. But we must always remember that those who lived and worked in the 18th century were men and women of that era. They lived when *gens una sumus* was only just beginning to make inroads into a world that didn't yet have it. The transition from the regnant attitudes of 1500 to the *gens una sumus* of today was one of the most important developments in human history, but it could never have happened overnight. When we judge people of a transitional era, what matters is whether they advanced or instead obstructed the development of the modern consensus. If they took part in advancing it, we should be grateful to them and honor them—not treat them as evil merely because they were not yet fully modern figures.

That is precisely the mistake that vandals make when they pull down statues of 18th-century people, ostensibly because of their alleged racism, when many of those people actually helped advance the values that we all now live by. At the University of Edinburgh, for instance, the "David Hume Tower" was renamed in the wake of an online petition accusing him of racism, though he was plainly a key player in the development of forward-looking Enlightenment ideas. One simple question immediately undermines the radical narrative: where were the African, Asian, or native American devotees of *gens una sumus* in Hume's day? The answer: there weren't any. Those people were still living in the world of 1500, fearing or loathing all peoples other than their own. Virtually all of them were, by modern standards, unreconstructed racists, pure and simple. If radicals want to find something to condemn in the 18th century, let them look to the places where unapologetic racism showed no signs of weakening.

It is simply astonishing that one of the leading figures in the development of our modern value system is reviled because he's not modern enough. Much the same is happening with many other crucial figures of that transitional era, including several of America's Founding Fathers. Modernity is indebted to these trailblazing figures, yet today's radicals condemn them for not being perfect examples of the values that they were busy developing.

It bears repeating: transitional periods are imperfect ones, and we must always focus on the direction of an era's progress, not on its limitations as compared to the present day. What cannot be disputed is that the 18th-century moral debate took place in Britain, and then in America, but not elsewhere. In the Asia or Africa of those times, no societal transformations were being launched. Thus, no complex judgments need to be made with respect to those areas, no ambiguities are to be noted in the behavior of people who are in transition from one ideology to another, as we see in America and Britain with figures like David Hume, Thomas Jefferson, and George Washington.

The heart of the matter is that the woke ideologues who advocate pulling down statues embody everything that real historians must guard against. They appear incapable of doing the historian's job of carefully tracing the development of ideas and events. Why? Because what the radicals really want is to ransack history to find important people that they can condemn as racists, which they do without any understanding of the origin and development of the ideas and values they invoke. All the follies of wokeness reduce to this misunderstanding of the history of modernity.

A third major misconception consists in the persistent claim that the explorers of the Age of Discovery and the later colonial administrators were evil people who oppressed and abused other peoples and looted their cultures. They are vilified as racist imperialists who practiced genocide. This too is a misreading of history that has everything that matters backwards.

Let's recall once more that before the Age of Discovery the world contained, on the one hand, an extensive network of contiguous cultures that had circulated critical innovations from one to the other for thousands of years, and on the other hand, scattered cultures elsewhere that were isolated not only from that known world but from one another. Critical technological innovations that took place in the known world had not reached those isolated cultures, and for that reason they lagged behind in their development. The voyagers of the Age of Discovery at last brought these previously isolated societies into contact with the known world, and so set them on the path to modernity.

How can we find fault with the discoverers for this? It was inevitable that, sooner or later, these isolated cultures would be brought into the orbit of the known world. What had isolated them was the primitive state of travel in earlier times, but that isolation would inevitably end as the means of travel improved. The seafarers of the Age of Discovery can't be blamed for doing something that was bound to happen in time, but in any case, contact with the known world was, in the long run, much to the advantage of those previously isolated cultures.

It's perfectly true that native populations were devastated by common diseases brought by contact with Europeans, because they had never been able to develop the immunity to those diseases that Europeans had. But a severe short-term medical crisis of this kind was inevitable. The long-term medical consequence of contact with the known world, however, would be quite another matter. Modern medicine has doubled the life-spans of the discovered peoples, and it has greatly improved their health and well-being.

Living conditions would also advance as native cultures became part of the known world and acquired access to its innovations. The first example of this came almost immediately: when Cortés let his horses run wild in America, they were soon domesticated by native Americans and rapidly became an important part of the culture of several tribes. Improvements in living standards of these cultures would continue well into the future. They now have modern technology that has raised them from subsistence to prosperity. Today, native Americans live infinitely better than they did before the Age of Discovery. Their continued isolation would have prevented all of this. Why should we wish that on them?

The attack on the discoverers sometimes focuses on their attitudes: they thought of themselves as superior to the peoples they discovered. But why wouldn't they? How could literate cultures of the iron age not feel superior to cultures that were, technologically, thousands of years behind them? They had been the beneficiaries of every technological and societal advance made in the known world during those years. Woke radicals are living in a fantasy world if they think that they would not have had the same feelings of superiority.

One particularly influential assault on the Western world's sense of superiority is that of Edward Said, who in his trend-setting book *Orientalism*[4] tells us that Western ways of thinking about the Orient represent the creation of "the Other," which is scholarly jargon for the practice of comparing a foreign culture to one's own and judging it negatively. Orientalism, writes Said, is "a Western style for dominating, restructuring, and having authority over the Orient."[5]

It's difficult to see anything of substance behind the fashionable argot here. Does Said mean that Europeans saw Eastern cultures as backward compared to their own? But what else could Europeans have thought in those early stages of contact? Said writes as if only Europeans formed opinions of other countries that were colored by their own cultural attitudes. He doesn't stop to ask himself whether there were countries anywhere at the time that didn't hold biased views of other cultures. Did Eastern cultures really have the sunny attitude to Europeans that Said seems to assume? The historical record is quite clear on this point: they didn't. The Ottoman Empire is proof enough of that.

Said's book accuses the West of inventing caricatures of oriental people. Yes, but that's what people everywhere did with respect to foreign cultures before the modern era—they formed sketchy pictures based on limited knowledge and an assumption of their own society's superiority. This way of thinking was universal—until the development of *gens una sumus* as the prevailing ideology of the modern world. But it was Western, not Eastern, thinkers who brought that ideology about.

Said essentially charges Europeans with lagging other cultures in seeing foreign peoples in their own terms and learning to respect them as such. Yet, plainly, the exact opposite is true. It was Europeans who were the first to develop widespread curiosity and affection for foreign cultures. The 18th-century Turkish craze in Europe had no parallel outside the West. Said is so completely in the grip of a hostility to the West that he can't see what is obvious in the historical record: what he accuses the West of is far more widespread and virulent outside the West. Like other radicals, he attacks the West by appealing to values that are quintessentially Western.

Another complaint against colonialism was that colonizers enriched themselves by exploiting native peoples. In some cases, this was true: King Leopold II of Belgium, for example, bled his colonies dry to enrich himself. However, this was not even true of the Belgians more generally. And in the case of the largest and most important of all empires—the British Empire—it was largely not true. The British spent so much on infrastructure and on the machinery of good governance that in its later stages the British Empire was a net drain on the British economy. For Britain, it was eventually the added strength in world affairs afforded by its empire that was the motivating force for their continuing it. That was why the colonized peoples were somewhat better off for being part of the British Empire.

Still another complaint against European imperialism is that the Europeans snuffed out foreign religions and cultural customs by allowing missionaries to convert native populations. But this complaint demands something of the explorers that could never have been expected of anybody at the time. How could Christians not have regarded religions that demanded human sacrifice (including even the ritual murder of children) as cruel and primitive? Christianity is about redemption and mercy. What believer in the Ten Commandments would not have been revolted by cannibalism, torture, and the burning of widows? And what devout Christian would not have wanted the blessing of his great faith to be shared more widely?

The simplest response to this complaint is that most of the religious practices that the colonial administrators suppressed are now universally condemned in the modern world, having been long since abandoned by the native cultures. Those cultures have simply adapted to the modern values that the colonists brought to them. There is no longer support for the sacrificial killing of innocent people, ritual torture, or the consumption of human flesh. Why, then, complain about European explorers who outlawed such practices?

That the Europeans used force to conquer native cultures is, again, something that could hardly have been otherwise, because this was a universal practice at the time. The age-old law of "bigger is better" (and safer) still prevailed, and every society did its utmost to extend its domain. This was the state of things before the Age of Discovery and for a long time after it. To find the first examples of people who became sufficiently concerned about the ethics of annexing other peoples to actually begin to shrink from it, you would need to look well beyond the Age of Discovery and into the future—to the British Enlightenment and its legacy. But even at that later time, the European nations who excelled at warfare were still using force to extend their domains. In other words, the rest of the world had similar ambitions, only more limited means of achieving them. This widespread practice of empire-building was not ended by the peoples of Asia, nor of Africa, nor of the pre-Columbian

Americas. What ended it was the ideology of *gens una sumus*. To insist that one nation not subjugate another is to employ an idea first put into practice by those much-reviled British.

As we've noted above, empires existed in every corner of the globe, and among every population group—including Africans, Asians, Europeans, and native Americans. Yet only one empire can be distinguished from the others in that it ended not by military defeat but by the voluntary action of the colonizers: the British Empire. They did so because the ideology of *gens una sumus* was inconsistent with imperialism. That viewpoint is now the basis of a worldwide orthodoxy as to the wrongness of empire. If we let the main outline of world history, rather than the narrow perspective of modern radicals, guide our judgment, the British can be seen as who they really are: not typical imperialists, but rather the people who ended imperialism.

Certain holdouts still advocate imperialism, but they do so by defying the worldwide orthodoxy. Most are insulated from the bitter criticisms levied at the British Empire because they are largely Marxist. Communist China still holds onto Tibet, and the Russian Federation (now led by a former KGB colonel) still controls much of the old Russian Empire. But even these remaining colonial powers know that they must never publicly acknowledge that they still have empires. Russia and China enlarged themselves with territories adjacent to them, and they now claim that those territories are really part of their countries, not imperial conquests. But whatever the case for independence of Kurds, Basques, Catalans, Ukrainians, Tatars, or Tibetans, that case can never in principle be different from that of the Tongans. What defines a colonized people is not that you must get into a boat to get to them, but rather that they form a relatively distinct people that wishes to control its own affairs. The few holdout imperialists aside, it is now generally accepted that each distinct people has the right to control its own destiny. That consensus is not the reason for Britain's abandoning its empire, but the reverse. It's the result of British opinion and the decolonization that followed from it.

The end of empire has much in common with the end of slavery. There too, unique responsibility for something that had been practiced in almost every society in the world is commonly laid at the door of

Europeans, even though what is genuinely unique about Europeans is not their practicing slavery, but rather their ending it. Slavery was practiced worldwide, and empire was what every country hoped to achieve. Until the English-speaking world questioned the ethics of slavery and empire, those practices continued unimpeded—yet radicals vent their anger precisely on the people who led us away from those things. The root of the problem here lies in the radical Left's fixation on proving that White people are bad, and that non-White people are good. But that pair of opposites is not the right one to use as exemplars of right and wrong here. More appropriate would be a temporal contrast: earlier periods did not live by *gens una sumus*, but more recent ones have come to do so. And the driving force in bringing about that change was the Anglosphere.

A fourth misconception is really a special case of the third. It consists in the charge that European explorers and their descendants stole land from native peoples. What those who make this accusation don't grasp is that where the spirit of *gens una sumus* was absent and tribalism prevailed, occupation of land was a very different matter. Robert Edgerton provides some essential historical context: "Tribal societies in Africa, New Guinea, Polynesia, the Americas, and elsewhere now and then drove their enemies off their lands, and others fought desperate battles that involved appalling loss of life."[6] From time immemorial, the reality was that ownership of land rested on the ability of its occupier to defend it. Most would take their neighbors' land whenever they could. This meant that the map would be constantly changing as tribes moved.

This process was not confined to smaller tribal units. In Africa, Shaka expanded his Zulu empire substantially, not because he had any rightful claim to adjacent lands, but because he could. Muslim empires acquired vast new territories by conquest on the same principle.

Jeff Fynn-Paul gives a useful account of how this worked specifically in North America:

> In North America, most Natives were primitive farmers. This means that (with some exceptions) they had no permanent settlements: they farmed in an area for a few decades until the soil got tired, before moving on to greener pastures where the hunting

was better and the lands more fertile. This meant that tribes were
in constant conflict with other tribes. It also meant that chiefs
were continually vying for power, creating confederations under
themselves, and that the question of who owned the land was in
a more or less constant state of flux. In most of North America,
the idea that any one piece of land belonged to any one tribe, for
more than 50 or 100 years, is therefore highly questionable.[7]

Fynn-Paul's conclusion is trenchant: "The idea that the Europeans stole
some land which had belonged in perpetuity to any one tribe is therefore ludicrous."[8] Over much of the globe, then, occupation of land was
seen not in terms of rights, but of capabilities. Native American tribes
evidently saw the European settlers initially as just another tribe, sometimes leaving Europeans to themselves, sometimes contesting their
presence on land that they wanted for themselves, sometimes allying
with them against other tribes. The Pequots were almost annihilated not
because European settlers stole their land, but because they were hated
by other tribes (including the English) for their tendency to annihilate
others when they were trying to take their land. A coalition that included White settlers went to war against them. Once more, Fynn-Paul's
summary judgment is accurate: "What the Europeans did in the New
World was insert themselves into a fluid power struggle which had been
ongoing for millennia."

The crucial question for today's historians and scholars is how these
age-old attitudes came to change. The answer is that they changed only
with the spread of the ideology of *gens una sumus*.

Yet the most compelling argument against the stolen land claim is
the relative population density of the Americas. As Lewis Lord said in
1997, the true pre-1492 numbers for the population of the Americas
are "forever unknowable."[9] Estimates vary enormously, ranging from
Alfred Kroeber's 1937 estimate of 8.4 million[10] to Henry Dobyn's 1966
estimate of around 100 million.[11] Some ideological bias may certainly
be suspected in the enormous discrepancy between these figures: where
a good proportion of a population are hunter-gatherers, the kind of
population density that Dobyn's figure suggests seems highly unlikely.

But what is much less disputed is that the native population collapsed after contact with Europeans. Records suggest a post-collapse population of only 6 million.[12] The major cause of the collapse was the native population's lack of immunity to the communicable diseases brought by the Europeans.

After this collapse of native populations, the population density of the Americas became so low that it was no more than a tiny fraction of what that enormous land mass could support. In the context of so low a population density, Europeans surely did as anyone else would have done. It is completely unrealistic to suppose that such vast tracts of land would hold so few people for long.

The case of Australia and New Zealand is even more clear. New Zealand is twice the size of England, yet there were probably between one and two hundred thousand Māori living there before European settlement began.[13] (That's about one fifth the population of a single present-day regional British city such as Leeds.) The native population initially welcomed the Europeans because they immediately recognized that the new arrivals had things that they wanted and could trade for. A reasonable estimate of aboriginal population in Australia before Europeans arrived is about three quarters of a million people[14] (about the same as the present population of Leeds), but Australia is the world's sixth largest country, and nearly thirty times the size of New Zealand. In Tasmania, an island over half the size of England, there were only about five thousand people. These were all large territories with minimal populations, even before diseases reduced their populations substantially. For all these reasons, the moral outrage of modern ethnocentric ideologues about stolen land is clearly fabricated. At the time, nobody thought that land was being stolen, and it's safe to say that, had those complaining today been there, they too would have joined in.

A fifth major error concerns the way in which today's educational curricula are alleged to be racist and colonialist when they focus largely on Western history and Western scientific and artistic achievements. Reading lists associated with those curricula are said to be racist because they contain many more White than Black and Brown authors.

It's certainly true that White authors are heavily "overrepresented" (if compared to the world's overall population) in many courses and reading lists, but this is not because they were White. Rather, it's because they were the authors who developed our modern way of life, and the ones we should read if we wish to learn how they did so. Those reading lists are compiled not to advance White supremacy, but to equip students with a thorough knowledge of the history and nature of modernity—something that is urgently needed if they are to thrive in modern times. It's not a question of preferring one race to another. There will be relatively few Black authors on a reading list about the early development of modern knowledge, but that's unfortunately because few Black authors were involved directly in that development. It ought not to be controversial that a modern education should afford the student an awareness of how we got here, and what we have inherited from our predecessors. The mistaken zeal to represent all races equally in all things has already resulted in a great deal of ignorance, and students have been force-fed ideas about racism in the past that are simply false. What students are not being taught is the true story of how that racism was overcome.

If we bow to demands for the proportional representation of authors by race, that will mean dropping pivotal historical figures in order to include very recent authors who will likely have no lasting importance. Essential knowledge will be replaced by feel-good substitutes that are irrelevant to what students should be learning. Ground-breaking thinkers and writers who helped to create our modern world will be replaced by authors chosen not for their ideas, but for their racial identity. That will also give our children the false impression that books about race are the most important kind of books. They are decidedly not!

In the field of drama, choosing the best for study will obviously take us to Shakespeare. A Black student's education will be seriously handicapped if we allow radicals to deprive him or her of the greatest writer in the English language. The same will be true for English language novels: the rise of the novel in England happened when there were almost no literate cultures among the population groups that radicals want us to give proportional representation to. Those early novels must not be put out of bounds for students just because a racially diverse reading list for the 18th century is impossible.

The downgrading of Shakespeare is sometimes justified with the claim that he is a cheerleader for imperialism. The New Zealand Arts Council recently rejected funding for Shakespeare on this ground.[15] The claim is simply false: the British Empire didn't exist in Shakespeare's time. The first overseas settlement took place in North America in 1607, just nine years before Shakespeare's death. It's astonishing that the members of the New Zealand Arts Council appeared to know so little of this or any other empire, for there had already been hundreds of them by the time Shakespeare was writing. Even if Shakespeare had promoted a British Empire, he'd have been no different in that respect from any other person of his time. The idea that Shakespeare is implicated in empire is a specialty of Marxist critics, but the facts are clear: he had nothing to do with empire.[16]

One way to demonstrate that racism has nothing to do with the existence of the largely White reading lists for earlier periods is to contrast those lists with lists for more recent periods, still employing the same criteria of selection—that is, choosing the best and most informative works for each period. The reading lists for more recent times will look very different. In the 19th century there were few Black scientists and writers, and so choosing the most prominent and influential of that time naturally won't result in many Black names on reading lists. (A glorious exception is Alexandre Dumas, certainly among France's most-read novelists.) But because other races have been catching up recently, a list of the most important contemporary thinkers and writers looks a great deal less White. Tom Sowell is now acknowledged as an economist and political thinker of extraordinary distinction, and there are many other Black thinkers that now command attention. In the modern world, therefore, there's no need of racial quotas to get racially balanced reading lists: just picking the very best people will automatically give us racial diversity. But when studying the best writers from eras when literacy was well established in Europe but not in Africa and elsewhere, achieving the same racial diversity will be impossible. Imposing equity in those circumstances will shortchange Black and White children alike, because it will withhold from them essential knowledge about our civilization.

If we were to do as radical activists recommend, we should close off much of the past, and that would leave a huge gap in our children's education. But that outcome, a shocking one to most people, is exactly what the radicals want. It's not just that token minority writers (necessarily very recent ones) are more important to them than wider knowledge of our civilization's development. The deeper reason is that the more children are ignorant of our past, the more vulnerable they will be to distortions that portray our civilization as one long rule of evil. And this will, in turn, make them more likely to swallow the notion that civilization must be radically remade to correct that evil. A philosophy of education that positively requires ignorance of the past condemns itself.

The mistaken idea that traditional college reading lists are racist has unfortunately been made more plausible by a consistent mistake on the part of traditional scholars. The popular name for courses that trace the development of modern life has been "Western Civilization." But that title is neither accurate, nor does it focus our attention on what should be the real point of those courses. Mesopotamia is not in the West, but that is where agriculture probably started, and it's also the site of the first recorded code of government. Israel is not Western, yet the Jewish bible has been one of the most profound influences on modern thought and culture. India—again, not Western—is also part of our development. The first written grammar of any language was of Sanskrit, and that grammar is also one of the first treatises ever written. India's caste system had at its apex not princes but men of learning—scholars. China is not in the West, but gunpowder—invented by the Chinese—has been highly important for the development of modern life.

The proper title for these courses should instead be: "The Origins and Development of Modern Life." Had these courses been properly named, the radical attack on them could not so easily have succeeded. Because the conventional title suggested that they were all about the West, it was easy to object: why not include more about the rest of the world? With the more appropriate title, we'd make clear what these courses have always been about: how modern life developed. With that title, radical allegations of their racism would be much less plausible.

Another benefit of this more accurate labeling would be that the criteria for inclusion or exclusion of material for such courses would become clearer. Choices would be determined by the extent to which books concerned key events and developments that led us in the direction of our modern way of life. If a disproportionate number of European books are included, that decision must be justified, or not, according to a single consideration: are these books crucial to understanding how the modern world came to be? Once the rationale for these courses is more clearly stated with a more appropriate title, it will immediately become obvious that proportional racial representation is a frivolous irrelevance. A list of books faithful only to the story of our civilization's progress can't be racist.

The sad truth is that the radical political activists that now dominate our universities choose books for reasons that have nothing to do with historical fact. They are concerned only to keep students away from books that embody a value system different from their own. The irony here is that we'll only fully understand their radical ideology when we are able to set that system of thought in the context of its historical origin and subsequent development. That process would of course have to cover those many episodes when it proved to be disastrous.

What radicals are most concerned to avoid are books that show how particular historical figures gradually and often heroically developed our modern world and values. Those are the books we ought most of all to read to understand how our society developed. Mark Twain's *Huckleberry Finn* is a particularly valuable book in this respect, but teachers are now afraid to assign it because it contains words that make us uncomfortable. Edgar Wallace's *Sanders of the River* stories show us what one transitional period of history was really like, but they are now hastily being removed from library shelves. Wallace's portrayal of a benevolent district supervisor in Africa tells us a great deal about the transformation of the British Empire into a commonwealth of independent nations, and as such is a fascinating illustration of a significant stage in our development. Yes, it's true that certain books from the past (certainly those by Mark Twain and Edgar Wallace) contain things that, if said today, we would find offensive, but we all need to understand how those now-grating expressions were a meaningful part of historical conditions that are now gone. Contrary to what the radicals want us to believe, there were a great many good and honorable people among our ancestors. Even the radicals would have done much as they did if they had been born among them.

A sixth misconception is especially destructive. This one concerns how we should go about remedying the inequalities that have resulted from the way in which modernity developed, above all the unequal standing of different racial groups. Because radicals think that those inequalities derive from White greed, theft, and racism, the solutions they favor involve enforcing equal outcomes with respect to almost everything: jobs, college admissions, money, and so on. And if the inequalities of modern life had indeed been the result of theft and greed, we might well want to give back what was stolen. But this account of the origin of the disparities seen in modern life is utterly false.

The true history of those inequalities is the one I've given in this book: they result from unequal roles in the creation of modernity. Those most involved in creating innovations benefited from them first. Whites didn't steal this civilizational advance from others—they invented it, and they made it possible for others to enjoy it. Radicals see one racial group taking something from another, when what really happened was the other way around: the supposed takers in reality gave something to every other group.

Just as the radical solution to inequality follows directly from a faulty account of how inequality developed, so a more accurate and realistic account points in a quite different direction. The most sensible and productive plan for those belonging to population groups that were not among the innovators is to catch up as quickly as they can—to grab the innovations that constitute modernity with both hands, master them, and go on armed for better things. In the modern world, we are in a position to know that this approach really works. Asian-Americans, for instance, have left us in no doubt of this. They are now overrepresented in colleges and universities as well as in many other places of high achievement—even symphony orchestras. And outside the United States, Asians are doing much the same: Toyota now sells more automobiles in the U.S. than Ford, and the Korean firm LG ranks highest in customer satisfaction in the U.S. across all appliance categories. According to the financial magazine *Barron's*, Taiwan Semiconductor is now the world's most important chip maker. But this is exactly what one would normally expect: people who are catching up know that they must make a real effort to do so, and the result is that they develop a head of steam that soon propels them beyond everyone else and into the lead. This is a positive program for people who start off lagging behind the innovators. Asians evidently don't care who originated modernity—they care only about participating in it to the full, which they do.

So why isn't everyone proceeding just like the Asians? Well, African-Americans, for instance, suffer from one very serious disadvantage. For them, there is indeed now an oppressor class. No, not Whites: this oppressor class is the radical Left. Radicals tell them to see these far-reaching changes not as the development of modernity that benefits everyone, but as White supremacy, which they should reject. Logical reasoning, they say, is White hegemony at work. Objectivity—the very idea of "getting the right answer"—is White oppression. To read those thinkers and writers who were deeply involved in the development of modernity would be to bow to White dominance.

Nothing could be more destructive of Black prosperity than this advice. Astonishingly, it tells Blacks to avoid the highly successful path that Asians have taken. We should call this what it so plainly is: an evil sabotaging of Black progress. It is this attitude, not White supremacy, that is responsible for the persistence of Black economic hardship today. It encourages African-Americans not to put their efforts into mastering the conditions of modern life, but instead to sit on their hands, resenting modernity and all the mental and physical effort that went into producing it, as "Whiteness." And when because of this foolish advice so many Blacks predictably make little or no progress, they are encouraged to blame the people who gave them the precious new opportunities that they are not taking advantage of. Toyota didn't achieve its market dominance by abandoning logical reasoning and adopting woke mathematics. And planes crash if their designers don't "get the right answer." If Europeans had looked at the world this way in the distant past, they would have rejected agriculture because it was invented by Asians.

This advice that radicals now give Black students amounts to a retreat from modern values, and a rejection of *gens una sumus*. Instead of Blacks and Whites belonging to the same human family, they are now to be considered fundamentally different. There is White thinking and there is Black thinking. There is White science and there is Black science. Whites seek correct answers in mathematics, but Blacks should not. This is outright racism masquerading as anti-racism. It returns us to a place in history when the races were separate, and when it was assumed that one of those races was capable of things that the other was not. One wonders how people who promote this way of thinking can claim that they are the ones who think Black lives matter.

Affirmative action in college admissions has been the centerpiece of this destructive radical program that cripples Black progress. Over the years we've seen many critiques of racial preferences, and yet however cogent those critiques have been, radicals have almost always attacked them as racist without attempting to rebut them analytically.

The most compelling objection to racial preferences in education is that learning is very much a sequential business.[17] A student masters one stage before he can go on to the next, because each stage supplies the groundwork that makes learning in the next possible. Radicals interfere with that sequence by pressing Black students to jump stages—to go forward to a later stage before they have mastered the previous ones. Skipping stages means that those unfortunate Black students aren't able to succeed because they have been artificially promoted to a stage for which they have not laid the groundwork. Radicals persuade Black students that this is a promotion that they deserve, one that they are owed. But this is not a promotion at all, but rather an automatic road to failure. By this time, students who are failing because thrust into a stage they don't have the preparation for are easy prey for the radicals, whose aim is to create a large group of people who will bitterly resent the system that has failed them. These students are encouraged to blame Whites for their failure, not the radicals who are its real cause.[18]

There is a very simple remedy here: stop interfering in the natural development of students, and let them proceed at their own pace, which guarantees that they'll be ready for whatever stage they reach. But for this to happen we must not only sideline the destructive radicals who always press for policies that disrupt the development of Black students; another class of people will have to be reined in too, namely, the senior administrators who try to make themselves look good by increasing their minority student numbers. Those administrators expect applause for what they do, but they really deserve our condemnation. They are irresponsible people who sacrifice Black students so that they can enhance their own image.

We are not yet done with all the damage that racial preferences do. They also depress a student's motivation. In higher education young people must want to learn, and they must devote themselves whole-heartedly to it. They must want it enough to struggle for it. When radicals persuade Black students that they have a right to a place in a prominent university regardless of whether they have earned it, they send a highly damaging message: that Black students will be held to a lower standard than other people. And that will weaken their motivation to do the best they can.

Who has not panicked over an impending end-of-term examination and stayed up half the night studying? But when young people are told so many times that they are owed equal standing regardless of their scores, they won't strain as others will. What they lose thereby is not just mastery of a particular subject. Even more important is that they will lose a sense that their future depends on their own efforts. Their motivation will have been crippled. They'll lose out on intellectual growth and on a sense of achievement, and they'll never acquire the habit of rising to the occasion through sweat and tears. Instead, they'll learn that it's more comfortable and profitable to exploit racial guilt than to use their full mental capacity. Radicals complain that students of color are handicapped, but they themselves are the real handicap.

It is well attested that Asian students put in many more hours of study than White students, and that White students put in more hours than Black students. Most Black students enter college with much lower College Learning Assessment scores than their White counterparts, and that gap widens further during their college years, because they study less than White students.[19] This is no accident: it's what happens when you tell one group that they must work extra hard to succeed (the message currently sent to Asian students) while you tell another that they will be held to a lower standard (the message currently sent to Black students). Imagine a parent telling one of his children that great things are expected of him and that he'll be held to the highest standard, while a second child is told that he'll be held to a lower standard because less is expected of him. If we saw that happening, we'd naturally think: what does that parent have against his second child? This is obviously an unfit parent who is sabotaging one child's future. But that is exactly what radicals constantly do to Black students.

Still another dimension of the damage done by preferences is the undermining of a Black student's confidence. If that student finds himself in an environment where everyone is smarter or has higher test scores than he, feelings of inadequacy will start to sabotage his morale and consequently his work. Racial preferences push students into situations where feelings of inadequacy undermine their belief that they can succeed if they only try hard enough.

If we take all these factors together, it's clear that radical activists are taking a tremendous toll on Black success. Why are we allowing those radicals to do such damage? The answer appears to be that anyone who tries to call out or stop this destructive behavior knows that he will be denounced as a racist. We must not allow this tactic to succeed. When you see a radical trying to persuade young Black people that mathematical reasoning is Whiteness, you are certainly not seeing someone advancing social justice or Black progress. What you are really seeing is a political zealot willing to sabotage Black progress to advance his own political goals.

Radical activists know that if Black students were to master modernity as Asian-Americans are doing, they would become independent people, escaping the clutches of ideologues who want to recruit them to their cause of disrupting and dismantling our prosperous society. When they encourage young students to feel victimized by the fact that there are few Black 18th-century novelists on their reading lists—a fact which has a simple and benign historical explanation—they are keeping them from success.

Activists rely on a single word above all others to justify what they do: "oppression." But that's a word without any clear content. Words like "slavery" or "segregation" specify real things that happened in the past—real abuses. They leave us in no doubt as to the kind of evil that is being talked about. But "oppression"? That word is now used as a blanket accusation. Does it refer to the fact that Blacks are on average less prosperous than Whites? Or that they are incarcerated at higher rates than Whites? Those are specific assertions that can be investigated, evaluated, and explained. If Asians have low rates of incarceration and high rates of college success, while those figures are reversed for Blacks, we obviously need to find some specific "oppressive" action being taken against Blacks that is not being taken against Asians. In the absence of specific content, accusations of oppression are devoid of meaning.

Where does our society really stand now, with respect to matters of race? A look at the sweep of history from 1500 to the present ought to make us optimistic and confident. We have made enormous strides. The truth is that we've long since overcome the widespread fear and loathing of other cultures characteristic of 1500. We've progressed especially in the last seventy-five years, during which we have become a multi-racial society in which all kinds of people work well together and have valuable friendships. This represents a complete transformation of our society's attitudes to race if we compare those attitudes to, say, the situation before World War II. But leftist radicals don't want to notice this heartening progress, because doing so doesn't serve their purposes. The one thing they can't abide is a society that thrives on free markets and is confident in itself. Only an unhappy society will consent to radical transformation.

Well-functioning modern governments have all undergone a gradual evolution in which they have slowly become more responsive to their peoples. Since at least the ancient Greeks, a great deal of thought on democratic forms of government has taken place, and modern countries have clearly learned a great deal from that extensive body of thought.

The best example of this is surely the United States Constitution. But the socialist regimes of the modern world have ignored that complex and fascinating legacy of political thought, and instead have taken their countries back to primitive forms of tyranny. North Korea is now essentially a military dictatorship with an absolute monarchy. The same has been true of Cuba. Both call themselves "democratic," but that is an Orwellian use of a word to mean the reverse of what it really says. The communist regimes of Mao and Xi are throwbacks to the days of the arbitrary rule of the all-powerful Chinese emperors. The same is true of Putin's Russia that has begun to resemble the country of Lenin, Stalin, and Brezhnev, all of whom have far more in common with the autocratic Tsars than with administrators of modern democracies.

These regimes that our radicals now appear to admire represent a regression to a time before there was any discussion of the tyranny of the majority; of checks and balances and the limits of government power; of the importance of a free press; of the need for an independent judiciary; of the need for free speech and assembly; and much more. Political radicals call themselves "progressives," but this too is an Orwellian usage that means the reverse of what it seems to say, because the societies they want to emulate are in reality severely regressive. They would take us back to primitive tribal societies governed by absolute leaders with unlimited power, and thus to a time before modern political thought began. No matter how many years they have spent on this earth, leftist radicals remain stuck in adolescent rebellion against their own societies, and in primitive ignorance of political history. Their ideas hurt everyone who believes in them—but especially those racial groups that should at this moment be putting their energies into catching up by mastering modernity.

This stunted political outlook is at the bottom of all the misconceptions I've diagnosed. It rests on a complete misreading of the historical development of modernity, and of how its ethos of *gens una sumus* developed. I have written this book in part to show that this radical misreading of history underlies a destructive agenda, and that a better understanding of how we got from 1500 to the present day is the antidote we need.

The delusions I've discussed in this chapter are now dangerously influential. To illustrate this, let me cite a policy statement recently offered with great pride by a major department of an American university. It is typical of what now passes for enlightened thought in academia:

> The Department of English at the University of Houston-Downtown recognizes the sovereignty of Tribal Nations and stands on the grounds of the Akokisa, Atakapa-Ishak, Coahuiltecan, Karankawa, and Sana peoples. We, the English Department, acknowledge that systemic racism harms Black and African-descendant, Indigenous, Latin American, Latinx and Latine, Asian, Asian American, American Arab, Middle Eastern, North African, and multi-racial persons, and we are all the worse because of it. We are aware that we are complicit in systems of oppression through our individual and collective actions. We reject white supremacy and its ideologies of racism, xenophobia, misogyny, homophobia, transphobia, and ableism. We uphold social justice in our lives and work as teachers and scholars. We embrace diversity, equity, and inclusion. . . . the English Department commits itself to the anti-racist work of 1) resisting and dismantling white supremacy and white supremacist ways of knowing and being in our educational practices; 2) creating spaces for historically racialized, marginalized, and silenced ways of knowing and being; 3) affirming and enacting education which attends to the material, contextual, and intersectional lives of our students, including robust curricula in all of our programs that gives voice and representation to the intersectional complexity of all people of color . . . we commit each day to working towards a better department that divests itself from the maintenance of white supremacy.

Let us hope that at some not-too-distant future time historians will look back at the absurdity of this typical product of our time and judge it as it should be judged—as a passing madness of crowds, comparable to so many other famously stupid episodes in human history[20] in which a delusion seized control of large numbers of easily led people. For only a collective madness could have generated these fantasies about the origin of anti-racist ideas, delusions about White supremacy as the source of all problems, pipe-dreams that enforcing equality of outcomes (that is, illegal racial quotas) will solve everything instead of making things very much worse, paranoia about ill-defined "oppression," and hallucinations about racism getting worse instead of now being greatly reduced.

The statement that I've cited happens to originate with the department of English at the University of Houston, but it scarcely differs from similar proclamations now being made throughout our system of higher education. The prevalence of such statements amounts to a shocking indictment of the historical ignorance that now prevails in academia.

The story I have told in this book—of the origin and development of modern attitudes to other peoples and races—is at odds with everything that the political radicals who now control our colleges and universities believe. They think that modernity is riddled with racism; the truth is that modernity has rescued us from racism. They think that capitalism is heavily implicated in racism, but history shows that it was free markets that gave us anti-racism. They think that Europeans are the villains of the story, but history tells us that they are its heroes. They think that the world would be sweetness and light without the corrupting influence of Western society, but the truth is that the world was a swamp of racism and nastiness until it was led out of those evils by the Anglosphere. They think that they, the radicals, are leading us to a more just and anti-racist world, but the truth is that they are returning us to racist chaos. They think that modernity needs to be destroyed so that we can reach racial nirvana, but the truth is that they would destroy a precious multi-racial society in which, for the first time in history, different races live side by side in harmony.

Notes

Introduction

1. Robert B. Edgerton, *Sick Societies: Challenging the Myth of Primitive Harmony* (New York: Free Press, 1992).

2. Even the chess world has not always been able to keep to the spirit of *gens una sumus* at the chessboard. In 1951 the British Chess Federation staged what was to be a world-class tournament to commemorate the celebrated London tournament of 1851 that had been part of the British Exhibition. All the world's greatest players were invited. One of them was the distinguished Yugoslav player Svetozar Gligoric, but the invitations were sent out not long after the 1948 expulsion of Yugoslavia from the Cominform. That had happened because Yugoslavia had just begun to go its own way rather than as Stalin directed. Accordingly, the British were informed that if Gligoric were invited, the Soviet Union would not permit players from the U.S.S.R. or from any of the east European satellite countries to participate. The British refused Stalin's terms. As a result, a rather sad tournament that lacked almost all the world's leading players was won by Gligoric, with two fellow Yugoslavs taking the next two places. It was not the first time, nor would it be the last time, that chess players didn't act like members of the same family.

3. For example, Nikole Hannah-Jones, et al., "The 1619 Project." *New York Times Magazine*, August 14, 2019.

Chapter One

1. Edgerton, *Sick Societies*, 94, 100.

2. Edgerton, *Sick Societies*, 70–71.

3. Theodora Kroeber, wife of the great anthropologist Alfred Louis Kroeber, wrote a much-admired account of Ishi and his tribe: *Ishi in Two Worlds* (Berkeley and Los Angeles: Berkley Books, 1961).

4. Edgerton, *Sick Societies*, 92.

5. Edgerton, *Sick Societies*, 148, 161. Edgerton records many examples of this usage, for example by the Hopi, Maasai, Maori, and Yahi.

6. Peter H. Wilson, *The Thirty Years War: Europe's Tragedy* (Cambridge, MA: Belknap Press, 2009), 790.

7. Hajo Holborn, *A History of Modern Germany 1648–1840* (Princeton: Princeton University Press, 1964), 23. Estimates of deaths during the Thirty Years War are complicated by at least two major factors. First, it is never clear whether increases in population numbers that could have been expected during these thirty years should be added to the losses. Second,

it is also never clear how much the figures for deaths should be reduced
by the numbers of those who may have fled from the area.

8 Wilson, *The Thirty Years War*, 4.

9 Edward Said devotes an entire book to this foolish accusation: *Orientalism*
(New York: Pantheon Books, 1978).

10 A convenient and complete overview of life expectancy in different eras
and areas is Wikipedia's "Life Expectancy" article: "Life expectancy,"
Wikipedia, last modified February 8, 2024, accessed February 20, 2024,
https://en.wikipedia.org/wiki/Life_expectancy.

Chapter Two

1 Niall Ferguson, *Empire: The Rise and Demise of the British World Order and the
Lessons for Colonial Power* (New York: Basic Books, 2002), 193. Ferguson
believes that even Ireland was brought under British control mainly to
stave off the danger that "Roman Catholic Ireland might be used by Spain
as a back door into protestant England." *Empire*, 47.

2 "List of Empires," Wikipedia, last modified February 20, 2024, accessed
February 23, 2024, https://en.wikipedia.org/wiki/List_of_empires.

3 Ferguson, *Empire*, 188.

4 David Lewis, *We, the Navigators: The Ancient Art of Landfinding in the Pacific*
(Honolulu: University of Hawaii Press, 1972).

Chapter Three

1 George H. Sabine, ed., *Milton: Areopagitica and Of Education: With
Autobiographical Passages from Other Prose Works* (New York: Appleton-
Century-Crofts, 1951), ix.

2 Daniel Hannan, *Inventing Freedom: How the English-Speaking Peoples Made the
Modern World* (New York: Broadside Books, 2013), 140.

3 Gertrude Himmelfarb, *The Roads to Modernity: The British, French, and
American Enlightenments* (New York: Knopf, 2004), 25.

4 Himmelfarb, *The Roads to Modernity*, 170

5 David Hume, *A Treatise of Human Nature* (London: John Noon, 1739; Project
Gutenberg, November 24, 2022), Book III, Part II, Section VIII: "On the
Source of Allegiance," https://www.gutenberg.org/cache/epub/4705/
pg4705-images.html#link2H_4_0095.

6 John Wesley, *Thoughts Upon Slavery* (London, 1774), 34–5, 52.

7 Hannan, *Inventing Freedom*, 286.

8 Ferguson, *Empire*, 106.

Chapter Four

1   David Hume, "Of the Original Contract," *Essays Moral, Political, and Literary* (Indianapolis: Liberty Fund, 1985), 467–68.

2   Hannan, *Inventing Freedom*, 255–6.

3   John M. Ellis, *Literature Lost* (New York: Yale University Press, 1997), 102.

4   Hannan, *Inventing Freedom*, 241, 213.

5   Bruce Gilley's "The Case for Colonialism" was reprinted in *Academic Questions*, 31, Summer 2018, 167–85. His subsequent article, "The Case for Colonialism: A Response to my Critics," was published in the same journal, 35, Spring 2022, 89–126.

6   "The Indian Army in the Second World War," The Commonwealth War Graves Commission, archived webpage accessed February 20, 2024, https://web.archive.org/web/20160619233546/http://www.cwgc.org:80/foreverindia/context/indian-army-in-2nd-world-war.php.

7   Zareer Masani, "'Every Effort Must Be Made'," *Finest Hour* 191, International Churchill Society, First Quarter 2021, 27, accessed February 20, 2024, https://winstonchurchill.org/publications/finest-hour/finest-hour-191/every-effort-must-be-made/.

8   Cited by Daniel Hannan, *Inventing Freedom*, 297.

9   Ferguson, *Empire*, 306.

10   Gilley, "The Case for Colonialism," 172.

11   Gilley, "The Case for Colonialism: A Response to My Critics," 105

12   Gilley, "The Case for Colonialism," 168.

13   Estimates vary, but these are the numbers given by the International Military Tribunal for the Far East, a military trial convened on April 29, 1946, to try leaders of the Japanese Empire for these crimes: "Basic Facts On The Nanking Massacre And The Tokyo War Crimes Trial," The Research Centre for Humanities Computing, The Chinese University of Hong Kong, 1990, accessed February 20, 2024, https://humanum.arts.cuhk.edu.hk/NanjingMassacre/NMNJ.html#nm.

14   Ellis, *Literature Lost*, 95–6. The cited material is from Barbara Crossette, "The Island that Fell From Grace," *New York Times Book Review*, 26 April 1992.

15   Gilley, "The Case for Colonialism," 176.

16   Ferguson, *Empire*, 106.

Chapter Six

1   The most prominent exponent of this foolish idea is Robin DiAngelo, as expressed in her *White Fragility: Why It's so Hard for White People to Talk about Racism* (Boston: Beacon Press, 2018). Equally guilty is Ibram X. Kendi (born Ibram Henry Rogers) in his *How to be an Anti-Racist* (New York: One World, 2019). Both make much of the idea of White privilege, and yet demonstrate no grasp of the role northern Europeans played in developing modernity, or of the degree to which that development has promoted the well-being of every people on earth.

2   This system of thought began with Derrick Bell's *Race, Racism, and American Law* (Boston: Aspen Publishing, 1970). At this stage the preferred name was "Critical Legal Studies," but during the 1970s that morphed into "Critical Race Theory."

3   Kendi formulated the most succinct version of this belief in a tweet sent on September 6, 2020: "Historically capitalism + racism are interlinked, which is why I call them the conjoined twins + historians like me call them 'racial capitalism' in the singular. But some self-described forms of 'antiracism' are not anti-capitalist, which in my book means they're not antiracism." Ibram X. Kendi (@ibramxk), "Historically capitalism + racism are interlinked," Twitter, September 6, 2020, 5:44 p.m., https://twitter.com/ibramxk/status/1302724276412387334.

4   Edward Said, *Orientalism* (New York: Pantheon Books, 1978).

5   Said, *Orientalism*, 3.

6   Edgerton, *Sick Societies*, 166.

7   Jeff Fynn-Paul, "The Myth of the 'Stolen Country': What Should Europeans Have Done with the New World?" *The Spectator*, September 26, 2020, accessed February 20, 2024, https://www.spectator.co.uk/article/the-myth-of-the-stolen-country/.

8   Graeme Wood goes even further, ridiculing the growing tendency to ritual announcements of the occupation of stolen land: Graeme Wood, "'Land Acknowledgments' are just Moral Exhibitionism," *The Atlantic*, November 28, 2021, accessed February 20, 2024, https://www.theatlantic.com/ideas/archive/2021/11/against-land-acknowledgements-native-american/620820/.

9   Lewis Lord, "How many People Were Here Before Columbus," *U.S. News & World Report*, August 18–25, 1997, 70.

10 Alfred Louis Kroeber, *Cultural and Natural Areas of Native North America* (Berkeley: University of California Press, 1937).

11   Henry F. Dobyns, "Estimating aboriginal population: an appraisal of techniques with a new hemispheric estimate," *Current Anthropology*, 7 (October 1966).

12   Lewis Lord, "How many People Were Here Before Columbus," 70.

13   John Victor Tuwhakahewa Baker, "Population, Population Trends, And The Census," in *An Encyclopaedia of New Zealand*, ed. A. H. McLintock, 1966, accessed online via newzealand.gov.nz, February 20, 2024, http://www.TeAra.govt.nz/en/1966/population.

14   This figure is my own extrapolation from wildly varying estimates that are either much higher or much lower. See the estimates given in Aaron O'Neill, "Population of Australia from 1800 to 2020," Statista.com, accessed February 20, 2024, https://www.statista.com/statistics/1066666/population-australia-since-1800/, and the very different estimates given in "Demographics of Australia," Wikipedia, last modified February 14, 2024, accessed February 20, 2024, https://en.wikipedia.org/wiki/Demographics_of_Australia.

15   See, for example, "New Zealand pulls funding for school Shakespeare festival, citing 'canon of imperialism," *The Guardian*, 14 October, 2022, accessed February 20, 2024, https://www.theguardian.com/world/2022/oct/14/new-zealand-pulls-funding-for-school-sheilah-winn-shakespeare-festival-citing-canon-of-imperialism#:~:text=New%20Zealand's%20arts%20council%20has,%E2%80%9Ca%20canon%20of%20imperialism%E2%80%9D.

16   A prominent example is Stephen J. Greenblatt, *Renaissance Self-Fashioning: From More to Shakespeare* (Chicago: University of Chicago Press, 1980).

17   A related but also compelling argument is presented by Richard II. Sander and Stuart Taylor, Jr., in their *Mismatch: How Affirmative Action Hurts Students It's Intended to Help, and Why Universities Won't Admit It* (New York: Basic Books, 2012).

18   My essay "Starting Down the Slippery Slope," in *A Dubious Expediency: How Racial Preferences Damage Higher Education*, eds. Gail Heriot and Maimon Schwarzschild (New York: Encounter Books, 2021) documents some heart-breaking cases.

19   This research was done by Richard Arum and Josipa Roksa and is reported in their book, *Academically Adrift: Limited Learning on College Campuses* (Chicago: University of Chicago Press, 2011). See especially Chapter 3.

20   The classic treatment of the madness of crowds is by Charles Mackay: *Extraordinary Popular Delusions and the Madness of Crowds* (London, 1841).

Index

euthanasia, 66

exploration and travel: automobiles and, 2, 74, 75, 100; aviation, 75; exposure to other cultures, 2–3, 4, 20, 21, 27, 74, 77; modes of, 2–3, 55, 75; primitive standards of, 5–6, 15, 18, 55, 87; railroads, 2, 61, 66, 74, 75, 83; steam-powered, 2, 74

famine, 68, 72

farming methods, 18–19, 28, 66, 71, 76–77, 92–93, 97, 101

fear of others, 5, 6, 8, 10, 11, 13, 14, 19, 37, 56, 66, 86

Ferguson, Niall, 23

fiction, impact on society, 41–42, 95–96

films and movies, 2, 3, 75

food security, 7, 12, 13, 72

foreign cultures, growth in knowledge of, 2–4

Founders, American, 6

France, 5, 10, 11, 21, 28, 40, 41, 42–43, 55, 63

free press, 40, 105

free trade, 43–44, 48

Fynn-Paul, Jeff, 92–93

gens una sumus: Age of Discovery and, 17; British Empire and, 52, 59, 68, 70, 91; defined, vii; development of, 15–16, 24, 35, 38, 70, 71; literacy and, 71; Locke on, 46; missionaries and, 62; as modern luxury, 14; modern understanding of, 84–85; radicals' modern rejection of, 101; replacing tribalism, 55; slavery and, 38; warfare and, 13–14

German Renaissance, 44

Germany, 5, 10, 11, 12, 41, 44

Ghandi, Mohandas, 65

Gilley, Bruce, 66, 68

Glorious Revolution of 1688–89, 40, 72

government, limited, 27, 40

Great Britain. *See also* British Empire: as multi-racial society, 19; slavery, public opinion on, 47–48, 50–53, 55–58; superiority, feelings of, 28–29

Greeks, ancient, 27, 39, 46, 77, 104

gunpowder, 18, 19, 29, 97

Gutenberg, Johannes, 1, 3, 37, 39

Hannah-Jones, Nikole, 6, ix

Hannan, Daniel, 41, 60

Hastings, Warren, 47, 58

healthcare, modern, 14, 30, 76–77, 88

Henry VIII, 39

high colonial period, 33, 36

higher education, American, ix–x. *See also* education

Himmelfarb, Gertrude, 43–44

history, racial and moral judgments, 9, 16, 30, 30–33 (*passim*), 33–36 (*passim*), 38, 46–47, 62, 82, 86, 87–88, 91, viii, xi

Holborn, Hajo, 12

Huckleberry Finn (Twain), 98

humanity, shared. *See gens una sumus*

humans: physical adaptations of, 4, 5, 19, 20; racial and moral judgments of, 9, 16, 30, 30–33 (*passim*), 33–36 (*passim*), 38, 46–47, 62, 82, 86, 87–88, 91, viii, xi

human sacrifice, 30, 90

humans as one family. *See gens una sumus*

Hume, David, 35, 44, 51, 57–58, 86–87
Hundred Years' War, 28
hunter-gatherer societies, 28, 93–94
Hutcheson, Francis, 46–47
illiteracy. *See* literacy
immigration of non-Europeans, 5
imperialism, 23, 55, 58–60, 66–70, 87, 90–91, 96. *See also* British Empire
Incas, 23
India, colonization and, 47, 55, 61, 63, 64–65
Industrial Revolution, 66, 71–72, 73–78 (passim), 78, 85
infant mortality rates, 14
intellectualism, literacy and, 1–2, 37, 38–39, 47, 76
internal combustion engine, 74–75
International Chess Foundation, vii
international language, English as, 78–79
internet, 2, 3, 37, 75–76, 78, 79, 83
inter-tribal hostilities, 13
Inventing Freedom (Hannan), 41

Jefferson, Thomas, 32–33, 35, 87
Jews, literacy and theology of, 3, 27
judgments, racial and moral, 9, 16, 30, 30–33 (passim), 33–36 (passim), 38, 46–47, 62, 82, 86, 87–88, 91, viii, xi

Kant, Immanuel, 44
Kendi, Ibram X., 68, 84, 85
known world, defined, 17–18

land theft, misconceptions of, 92–94

language, English, 78–79
law and order, modern, 14–15
League of Nations, 79
Leibniz, Gottfried Wilhelm, 44
life expectancy, 14, 72
lingua franca, 78, 79
literacy: electricity and, 76; France and, 43–44; *gens una sumus* and, 71; growth of, 3, 36, 37–39, 40, 41, 42–43, 72; illiteracy, 28; influence of, 1, 52, 57; intellectualism and, 1–2, 37, 38–39, 47, 76; Jews and, 3; printing press and, 1, 3, 37, 38, 39; prosperity and, 39–40; in sub-Saharan Africa, 36
Literature Lost (Ellis), 59, 67–68
living standards, 38, 72, 72–76 (passim), 73–74, 88
Locke, John, 44–48
longbows, development of, 28–29
Louis XIV, 10

magazines and newspapers, development of, 1, 37, 39, 41, 57
Magna Carta, 27, 39, 40, 72
Marconi, Guglielmo, 3
Marxism, 84, 91, 96
mathematical reasoning, 103
medical care, modern, 14, 30, 76–77, 88
medicine, 30, 76–77, 88
Mesopotamia, 27, 77, 97
metallurgy, 18, 19, 28
Metternich, Klemens von, 11
Middle East, 14, 78, 106, viii
Midway, Battle of, 31–32
migrations, historical, 4, 5, 20
Milton, John, 40
missionaries, Christian, 33, 62, 90